TA̲ ̲ ̲ ̲ ̲ ̲ ̲ OF JOYCE

Talking of Joyce

Umberto Eco
Liberato Santoro-Brienza

edited by
Liberato Santoro-Brienza

University College Dublin Press
Preas Choláiste Ollscoile Bhaile Átha Cliath

First published 1998 by University College Dublin Press,
Newman House, St Stephen's Green, Dublin 2, Ireland

ISBN 1 900621 13 4

Publication of this book has been sponsored by the
Istituto Italiano di Cultura, Dublin

Cataloguing in Publication data available from the British Library

Typset in 12/13 Garamond by Seton Music Graphics, Bantry,
Co. Cork, Ireland

Printed in Ireland by Betaprint, Dublin

Contents

Preface and Acknowledgements   vii
Liberato Santoro-Brienza

Foreword   1
Italian-Irish Celebrations
J.C.C. Mays

A Portrait of the Artist as a Bachelor   7
Umberto Eco

Joyce's Dialogue with Aquinas, Dante, Bruno,
Vico, Svevo . . .   41
Liberato Santoro-Brienza

Preface and Acknowledgements

On 31 October 1991, Umberto Eco presented a paper at University College Dublin, to celebrate James Joyce on the anniversary date of his conferring as a Bachelor of Arts. The lecture was given in the Physics Theatre of the College, at its original address in Earlsfort Terrace, that Joyce had frequented. It was one of the events organised by the James Joyce School, under the enthusiastic direction of Augustine Martin, Professor of Anglo-Irish Literature and Drama at UCD. Four years later, on 25 October 1995, I gave a talk on 'Joyce and some Italian connections', at the James Joyce Cultural Centre, in Dublin.

Tragically and prematurely, Gus Martin died suddenly on the fifteenth day of that same month of October 1995. Lamenting the loss of our friend and colleague, we agreed to dedicate to his memory the publication of our lectures.

Many have to be thanked for the realisation of this project. First of all, I am grateful to Umberto Eco, for his generous encouragement and for readily entrusting me with the care of his text. The reader will be particularly grateful to him for making more permanent and more widely accessible – through the pleasure of reading – what was originally an eventful happening and an inspiring experience of listening. (We have intentionally chosen to preserve the original tone and character of our occasional lectures, certain that their oral intonation would not diminish their informative value.) I hasten, then, to express a vote of thanks and appreciation to Jim Mays, Professor of Modern English and American Literature at University College Dublin, for his elegant and delightfully congenial introductory note.

My special thanks to Ken Monahan, nephew of Joyce and Director of the Joyce Cultural Centre, and to the Italian Cultural Institute in Dublin, for their joint initiative which made possible my talk at the Centre. The Italian Cultural Institute and its Director, Dr Laura Oliveti, must also be thanked for their generous financial help towards the realisation of this publication. To acknowledge fully the Italian contribution to this project, I shall not fail to express my gratitude to our Italian Ambassador in Ireland, Dr Ferdinando Zezza, for his enthusiastic encouragement.

I must, finally, acknowledge my debt of gratitude to the friends who have assisted my editorial labours. I am particularly grateful to my wife, Mary, and my children Louisa and Giuseppe, for their unfailing and inspiring affectionate encouragement, and for having improved the early versions of the lectures; and I am deeply indebted to Patrick Gallagher, Professor of Spanish at University College Dublin, for his final revision and skilled refinement of the texts by Eco and myself. Of course, any trace of inelegance or any mistake that may be found in the printed text will have to be attributed solely to the editor.

I am grateful to the friends and colleagues who have helped and participated in this project, also because they have contributed to making this publication an appropriately – or should I say 'commodius'? – 'riverrunning' intercultural Irish-Italian celebration.

Liberato Santoro-Brienza
San Marino–Bologna–Milano–Roma–Dublin, 1995–97

Foreword
Italian-Irish Celebrations

Umberto Eco's opening words strike a note which is easy, informed and challenging; 'but then', he says, 'I am only a playboy of the southern world'. His lecture, and Liberato Santoro-Brienza's lecture which follows, engage us because they manifest encounters between minds of similar cast, on terms which, though forever respectful of Joyce, treat him on equal terms. Joyce is honoured by being engaged, argued against and sympathised with. He provokes lines of enquiry which are shown to be worth following and to have produced jokes worth capping. These two lectures do not embalm him as an exegete of postcolonial politics or a solemn guardian of the former avant-garde, as does so much Anglophone commentary. Nor is he positioned at the centre of a meta-physical universe *en abyme*, as in the French *nouvelle critique* of yesteryear. Eco and Santoro-Brienza take him on familiar terms as simply Jim, and they get directly to points which are worth discussing.

There are inevitably academic studies of Joyce and Italy – monographs on Joyce and Rome, on Joyce in Trieste, on the influence of Dante, in particular – and they are useful for their footnotes. The two encounters represented here possess a different value, which is – I say again – a particular quality of engagement. Eco and Santoro-Brienza are secure in the knowledge that their Jim spoke Italian in his family life to the end of his days. It was the language he used for what was nearest to him, even while others beyond the family-circle were speaking in German, French or English. He constructed his books in English, he spoke French and German to taxi drivers, but Italian remained the medium of his ordinary and most intimate living.

Santoro-Brienza acutely remarks that the Italian experience shaped Joyce's adult perception of 'ways of living, eating, being aware of one's bodily organs and expressing or deploying one's body'. Dubliners may feel they have a similarly privileged access to their author, though their advantage becomes an impediment when they forget why he preferred to live abroad. It seems to me that Eco and Santoro-Brienza strike an exact balance. They are sensitive to the ordinary in Joyce as they are also intimate with the broader sweep of his ambition. They register, even in the way they conduct their argument, how abstraction counters earthiness, in Joyce's mind, in tragicomic equipoise.

It is important that these lectures were given in Dublin. What repelled Joyce about Rome and whatever he found specially congenial in Trieste grew from seeds carried from the city he left. The same quality, amplified, which these lectures bring back has been, in turn, reflected by, moulded by, the audiences they addressed. The occasions were popular and of a sort Joyce would have approved. Umberto Eco's was given in the Physics Theatre in University College Dublin, at the invitation of the late Professor Augustine Martin; Liberato Santoro-Brienza's at the James Joyce Centre in North Great George's Street, which is benevolently presided over by Senator David Norris. Both places are cherished for offering opportunities for the plain people of Dublin to take the measure of academic criticism; both organisers are (or, in Professor Martin's case, sadly, were) committed to a broad understanding of the author they celebrate. In short, Eco and Santoro-Brienza did not lecture to convert, nor simply to instruct. They found something of what they brought, and their lectures are a sharing and enlargement.

Liberato Santoro-Brienza did not travel far, physically. He has taught in the Department of Philosophy at University College Dublin for many years and is well known, also, for cultural and sociological interests which extend beyond philosophy. His description of Joyce's engagement with Aquinas, Dante, Bruno, Vico and Svevo traces a series of encounters which are as often surprising as they are intimate. Joyce was less interested in contemporary intellectual movements – for instance, in the argument about Futurism inaugurated by contemporaries like Marinetti and Giovanni Papini – than in the way ordinary Italians lived their lives. His intellectual identification with Dante and Bruno or, on a different level, with Svevo afterwards is perhaps less important than his simple appreciation of the 'often crazy, operatic and heroic-comic ways' of Italians on the street. The point is so simple that it is difficult for intellectuals to accept, but it is worth many books and Santoro-Brienza communicates it entirely.

Professor Eco does not require an introduction from me. All I can say is that he winds up the quality which both lectures share to a delightful pitch. He knows early European history so intimately, and Joyce so well, that the conjunction of the two interests sparks new insights on every page. Some insights are small, such as his suggestion concerning the identification of John F. Taylor in the context of *Finnegans Wake* pages 353–6. Others are suggestive of whole new areas of research, such as his remarks on Hisperic literature. The amplitude and variety of the references he brings to bear on Joyce are literally an illumination. Even when we might have itched to interrupt – to supplement what he says about Joyce's identification of Irish and Phoenician languages by calling attention to Charles Vallencey and Edward

Betham and (particularly, given Joyce's recorded interest) the related controversy over round towers involving George Petrie – we collaborate in a dialogue which is open-ended. The quality of great modesty in the face of all we cannot know leaves Eco's range of learning tentative and welcoming. The performance has qualities of joy one associates with opera – another link between Joyce and Italy – and it should perhaps be recorded (because it has passed into Dublin lore) that Professor Eco sang Joyce's favourite arias, after the supper following his lecture, to the great delight of other guests at the same Dublin restaurant, long into the night.

Both lectures share a quality of *filologia*, a word which is entirely distorted by our dull translation, *philology*. It involves an ability to move between registers which the English language must take different occasions to attempt, to soar from the telling (earthy) detail to the panoramic (cosmic) frame. For this reason, these commentaries, by Italians in English, on an author of books in English who preferred to speak in Italian, are a rich and illuminating conjunction. Read these lectures for the way they are, for they bring together two worlds. Their eminent authors do not stand on dignity: they communicate directly what is important. They have different things to say, but each celebrates values which Joyce held most dear.

J.C.C. Mays
University College Dublin

A Portrait of the Artist as a Bachelor

Umberto Eco

Bachelors

I should probably not be considered as the most suitable speaker to celebrate the anniversary of Joyce's BA award, particularly since an article in a 1901 issue of *St Stephen's* alleged that Joyce had been corrupted by ideas coming from Italy. Anyway, I did not exactly volunteer to give this lecture: the responsibility for the choice of speaker rests entirely with University College Dublin.

The title of my paper is *A Portrait of the Artist as a Bachelor*, and perhaps my intertextual joke is not so smart – but then, I am only a playboy of the southern world.

I would have liked to speak also of the times when Jim, at Clongowes Wood College, spelled out his age by saying: 'I am half past six'. But I shall stick to our topic of this occasion, and deal mainly with Joyce as a Bachelor.

What does 'bachelor' mean? As you know, in many contemporary studies on semantics 'bachelor' has become a shibboleth, since it has been handed down from author to author as a paramount example of an ambiguous term which has at least four different meanings. A bachelor is (i) a human adult male not yet married; (ii) a young knight serving under the standard of another; (iii) a holder of an academic degree conferred after successful completion of the first three years of a tertiary education, and (iv) a young male seal who has the misfortune of remaining without a mate during the breeding season. However, the great linguist Roman Jakobson once remarked that, in spite of their semantic differences, these four homonymic terms share a common feature of 'incompleteness' or 'unaccomplishment'. A bachelor is in any case somebody who has not reached a state of ripeness. The unmarried young man is not yet a mature husband and father, the page is not yet a fully fledged knight, the BA is not yet a Master or a PhD, and the unlucky and inexperienced young seal has not yet discovered the pleasures of sex.

Was our Jim, at the moment he left University College Dublin, a still unaccomplished Joyce? Certainly he was, in so far as he had not yet written the works without which he would have remained and would now be remembered only as an arrogant sophomore. I would like, however, to suggest that, at the end of his studies in this College, Jim was not so relatively unaccomplished as one might expect from a young graduate. For it was precisely during his college years that he lucidly outlined and mapped, in his early experimental and seminal writings, all the paths that he was to follow in the course of his mature years.

Jim started his curriculum in 1898, reading English under the guide of Father O'Neill (a pathetic fan of the Bacon-Shakespeare controversy), Italian with Father Ghezzi, and French with Edouard Cadic. It was a time of neo-Thomistic revival, with a practice or method of learning guaranteed to become the quickest way to misunderstand Aquinas. Despite the limitations of neo-Thomist interpretations and pedagogical applications, however, while still in College, and before the Pola and Paris *Notebook*, Jim understood correctly one quite significant and relevant truth. Apparently he told his brother Stanislaus that, to his mind, Aquinas was a very complex and profound thinker because what he said sounds like what common people say, or would say. And this remark seems to me to epitomise the best way to understand the very essence of Saint Thomas's philosophy.

The Beginnings

In his lecture on *Drama and Life*, read on 20 January 1900, at a meeting of the University College Dublin Literary and Historical Society,[1] Joyce announced what was to become the poetics of *Dubliners*.

Still I think out of the dreary sameness of existence, a measure of dramatic life may be drawn. Even the most commonplace, the deadest among the living, may play a part in a great drama.[2]

In *Ibsen's New Drama*, published on the first day of April in the *Fortnightly Review*, we encounter that basic idea of artistic impersonality that we shall ultimately find fully articulated in *A Portrait*. In Joyce's words, 'Ibsen . . . sees it [the work of dramatic art] steadily and whole, as from a great height, with perfect vision and an angelic dispassionateness, with the sight of one who may look on the sun with open eyes.' (*CW*, 65) As a counterpoint idea to this, the God of the *Portrait* stands 'within or behind or beyond or above his handiwork, invisible, refined out of existence, indifferent, paring his fingernails'.

In the lecture on *James Clarence Mangan*, addressed to the Literary and Historical Society of University College Dublin (15 February 1902), and later published in May in *St Stephen's*, we find the formulation of another important idea, according to which:

> Beauty, the splendour of truth, is a gracious presence when the imagination contemplates intensely the truth of its own being or the visible world, and the spirit which proceeds out of truth and beauty is the holy spirit of joy. These are realities and these alone give and sustain life. (*CW*, 83)

This is undoubtedly the first source of the notion of epiphany such as it was developed in the later works.

In *The Study of Languages*, a paper written during the matriculation course of 1898–99, we can find an uncanny announcement of the underlying structure of *Ulysses*, when the young author speaks of an artistic language which escapes 'from the hardness, which is sufficient for "flat unraised" statements, by an over-added influence of what is beautiful in pathetic phrases, swelling of words, or torrents of invective, in tropes and varieties and figures, yet preserving even in moments of the greatest emotion, an innate symmetry.' (*CW*, 27)

Likewise, in the same text, one can hear an anticipatory though remote echo of *Finnegans Wake*, as well as of the future reading of Vico, when Joyce says that 'in the history of words there is much that indicates the history of men, and in comparing the speech of today with that of years ago, we have a useful illustration of the effect of external influences on the very words of a race'. (*CW*, 28) Moreover, Joyce's basic obsession, the quest for an artistic truth through the manipulation of all the languages of the world, reappears in another line of this early essay, where Jim the freshman writes that 'the higher grades of language, style, syntax, poetry, oratory, rhetoric, are again the champions and exponents, in what way soever, of Truth'. (*CW*, 27)

If it can be said that every great author develops a unique seminal idea during the whole course of his/her life, this seems particularly evident in the case of Joyce: not yet a bachelor, he knew exactly what he had to do, and he told it, even though informally and naively, on these college premises. Or, if you prefer to put it another way, he decided to do in his mature life what he foresaw while studying in these very rooms. During his matriculation course, Joyce had an opportunity of deeply reflecting – among other matters – upon the representation of the sciences in Santa Maria Novella and decided that Grammar was to be considered as 'the primary science'. The rest of his life was devoted to the invention of a new grammar, and his quest for artistic truth became the quest for a perfect language.

The Quest for a Perfect Language

In the year in which Dublin is celebrated as the European Cultural Capital, it is worthwhile to reflect upon the fact that the quest for a perfect language has been for a long time, and still is, a typical European phenomenon. Europe was born out of a unified cultural nucleus (the classical world of ancient Greece and Rome), but soon underwent a process of linguistic, territorial and ethnic fragmentation and differentiation. The world of ancient

Greece and Rome was neither concerned about the problem of a perfect language, not burdened by multiplicity of tongues. The Greek *koiné* first, and imperial Latin later, provided a satisfactory universal system of communication, adopted and shared throughout Europe, from the Mediterranean basin to the British Isles. The two peoples that had invented, respectively, the language of philosophy and the language of law identified the structures of their languages with the structures of the human mind. In particular, the Greeks lived in the innocent certitude of being the only race endowed with the power of articulate language: of being, indeed, masters of *the Language*. We have learnt to deduce this much by the fact that, for them, the rest of the humankind – all the non Greek speakers, foreigners and aliens – were simply 'barbarians': in etymological terms, and with onomatopoeic resonance, those incapable of articulate speech and deprived of language, those who communicate by stuttering and babbling 'bar bar bar. . .'.

The fall of the Roman Empire marked the beginning of a period of linguistic and political fragmentation. Latin became corrupted and debased. The empire was invaded by the barbarians, with their obscure languages and their inordinate customs. Slowly, half of the Roman dominions became linguistically colonized by the Greek tongue of Byzantium, while part of Europe, with most of the Mediterranean basin, adopted the Arabic language. Finally, the dawn of the new millennium witnessed the birth of the new and diversified national tongues.

And it was at this very historical moment that Christian culture began to re-read, with heightened interest, the biblical pages on the *confusio linguarum*: that momentous event that took place during the construction of the Tower of Babel. Biblical interpreters began to wonder whether it was possible to rediscover or to re-invent a pre-babelic language, a language common to the whole of mankind, capable of expressing the nature of things through a kind of native homology between things and words. Such a quest for a system of universal communication took different directions, either by going back in time in an attempt to rediscover the language that Adam originally spoke with God, or by going forward, attempting to construct a language of reason endowed with the lost perfection of the language of Adam – in any case pursuing what was later to become Vico's ideal project to find a mental language common to all nations. Such a quest is still actively pursued today, on the one hand by the invention of international tongues such as Esperanto, on the other by various attempts to design an artificial language of the mind, shared by and accessible to both humans and computers.

However in the course of this quest there have been numerous cases in which individual investigators would cheerfully and confidently assert that the only perfect language was the one spoken by their own countrymen. For instance, in the seventeenth century Georg Philipp Hasdörffer maintained that Adam could not but speak German, since only in German could the 'radicals' perfectly represent the nature of things. (Almost four centuries later, Heidegger suggested that one can philosophise only in German). Antoine de Rivarol, in his *Discours sur l'universalité de la langue française* of 1784, asserted – *au contraire!* – that French is the only language in which the syntactic structure of sentences mirrors the very structure of the human mind, and that therefore it can claim to be the only logical language in the universe. (To strengthen his point, as it were, our French author pointed to the . . . obviously indisputable fact that German is too guttural, Italian too soft, Spanish too redundant and English too obscure!).

Dante

It is well known that during his studies at this College Joyce enjoyed reading Dante Alighieri and that he remained a fan of the Florentine poet for the rest of his life. We should note that all his references to Dante concern only the *Divina Commedia,* but there are reasons to believe that he was also familiar with Dante's ideas on the origins of language and with his intention to create a new perfect poetic tongue: a project fully articulated in *De Vulgari Eloquentia*. In any case Jim would have found in the *Divine Comedy* clear references to such a topic and, specifically, he would have encountered – in *Paradiso,* Canto XXVI – Dante's new version of the old debate concerning the theme of the Adamic language.

De Vulgari Eloquentia was written between 1303 and 1305, and thus before the *Divina Commedia.* Though structured in the form of a doctrinal treatise, in actual fact it is a self-commentary in which the author analyses his own methods of artistic production, which he implicitly identifies with the very model and exemplar of every poetic discourse.

According to Dante the plurality of 'vulgar' tongues, the *confusio* begotten by the blasphemy of the tower of Babel, was preceded by the sole existence of a perfect language through which Adam communicated with God and with which his descendants spoke to each other (*De Vulgari Eloquentia* I, iv, v, vi). After the babelic confusion (I, vii) the languages multiplied, first in the various geographical areas of the world and then within the area that today we would call Romance, where they came to be divided into the language of *si*: the language of *oc,* and the language of *oil* (I, viii). The language of *si,* or Italian, in turn, broke up into a multiplicity of dialects that sometimes varied – and still vary – even from one area of a town to another. This fragmentation is due to

the unstable and inconstant nature of man in his customs and verbal habits, both in space and in time. It is
precisely to counteract and somewhat smooth over these
slow but inexorable changes in natural language that the
inventors of grammar sought a kind of immutable
tongue that might remain identical in different times
and different places (I, ix). They came to identify this
with Latin as it was written and spoken in the Schools
during the Middle Ages.

Unlike his contemporary grammarians, however,
Dante pursued an understanding and a justification of
'vulgar' Italian, the language actually spoken by the
people. Thanks to his encyclopedic knowledge and his
poetic culture, and thanks to the numerous contacts he
established as an itinerant exile, he was in a position to
gain direct experience of both the variety of the Italian
dialects and that of other European languages. Hence
the objective of *De Vulgari Eloquentia* is to define a
'vulgar' tongue that would be most dignified and most
noble among all others. And so, in his treatise, Dante
first proceeds with a strict critical analysis of the various
Italian vernaculars, spoken at the time. However he is
quick to notice that the best poets – as governors and
custodians of their tongue – have, each in his own way,
distanced themselves from their regional vernacular
(I, ix-xv). This suggests the possibility of finding a 'noble
vernacular', a *volgare illustre* (where 'illustre' means enlight-

ening, in the sense of 'diffusive of light') worthy to take abode in the royal court of a national kingdom, should the Italians ever have one, and thus be considered a truly national language. It would be a vernacular of every Italian city and of none exclusively, a kind of prototype and model, which the best poets have tried to establish and with respect to which – as an ideal norm – all the existing vernaculars would have to be judged (I, xvi–xix).

Thus, to counteract the confusing proliferation of the numerous and different tongues, Dante proposes the adoption of a language akin to the language of Adam. It would finally correspond to the poetic language of which he proudly considered himself to be the founder. Such a perfect language, to which Dante gives chase, as if to a perfumed panther (I, xvi, 1, 4–5), appears every now and then in the works of those poets whom Dante considers great, but is as yet unshaped, uncodified, and its grammatical principles have not yet been explicitly articulated. It is with reference to the existing vernaculars, natural but not universal, and to Latin grammar, universal but artificial, that Dante pursues his dream of the restoration of an Edenic language at once natural and universal. But unlike, for example, the Renaissance search for an original Hebrew language, Dante intends to recreate the original condition with an act of modern invention. The noble vernacular, of which his poetic language aims to be the finest example, is the instrument with which a 'modern' poet can heal the post-Babelic wound.

This bold conception of his own role as the restorer of the perfect tongue explains why in *De Vulgari Eloquentia* Dante, instead of lamenting or condemning the multiplicity of languages, emphasises their almost biological strength, their capacity for renewal and change over time. For it is precisely on the basis of this linguistic creativity that he is able to set out to invent a perfect, modern, natural language, without going back into the past in search of lost models. If Dante had believed that the primeval language coincided with the Hebrew tongue, he would have opted to write in Hebrew. Obviously, he never entertained the thought of such a possibility because he was sure to be able to find again, through an improvement of the various Italian vernaculars, those linguistic universals of which Hebrew was, to his mind, only the most celebrated embodiment.

Many of the arrogant statements of the young Joyce seem to allude to a similar task of restoring, by his own poetic invention, the conditions of a lost perfect tongue, in order to forge '*the uncreated conscience*' of his race: a language that would not be arbitrary like the vernacular, but supremely necessary and eminently justified. In this sense, the young bachelor perfectly understood, in some mysterious way, Dante's idea and he pursued it – in his own terms – during the whole course of his life.

Dante's project, as well as every other project concerning the establishment of a perfect tongue, was a search for a language that would allow mankind's escape from the post-babelic labyrinth. One can, as Dante did, accept the positive plurality of languages. A perfect tongue, however, should be clear, perspicuous, and not labyrinthine. On the contrary, Joyce's project, as he progressively moved from his early Thomistic aesthetics to the world-vision expressed by *Finnegans Wake*, is really about overcoming the post-babelic confusion *by accepting and exploiting it.* Joyce did not try to go before or beyond the Tower, but rather wanted to live *inside it.* And allow me to wonder whether perchance the decision to start *Ulysses* from the top of a tower was an unconscious prefigurement of Joyce's final purpose of forging a *polygluttural* and *multilingual* instrument of communication as a melting pot representing and celebrating the triumph of the *confusio linguarum.*

Where can we find the remote sources of such a daring project and extraordinary plan?

Early Irish Grammarians

Around the middle of the seventh century AD, a grammatical treatise appeared in Ireland the title of which was *Auraicept na n-Éces*, that is – as I have been told – *The Precepts of Poets.*[3] The fundamental idea of this treatise is that in order to adapt the Latin grammatical model to Irish one must imitate the structures of the Tower of Babel: eight or nine (according to the various versions of the text) are the parts of the discourse – such as noun, verb, adverb, and so on – and eight or nine were the basic elements used for the building of the Tower (water, blood, clay, wood, and so on). Why this strange and elaborate parallelism? Because the 72 wise men of the school of Fenius Farrsaid, who planned the reconstruction of the first language born, according to them, ten years after the babelic confusion (and it goes without saying that this language was Gaelic), tried to build up a tongue which, like the aboriginal one, was not only homologous to the nature of things, and hence mirrored it, but was also designed to take into account the substance of every language born after the babelic confusion. Their project was inspired by Isaiah 66.18: 'I shall come, that I will gather all nations and tongues'.

The method they followed consisted in selecting what they considered to be the best of every idiom by dissecting the other languages, finally to combine the collected fragments in a new perfectly coherent structure. We are tempted to say that in doing so they operated like artists, if we accept Joyce's remark that 'the artist who could disentangle the subtle soul of the image from its mesh of defining circumstances most exactly and "re-embody" it in artistic circumstances chosen as the most exact for it in its new office, he was the supreme artist'. (*Stephen Hero*, 78).

The operation of 'cutting' or 'segmenting' – currently a fundamental operative concept in the explanation of linguistic systems – was so important for these 72 wise men that (as my source has informed me) the Gaelic word for segmenting, and therefore for selecting and modelling: *teipe*, came to denote antonomastically the Irish tongue as *beila teipide*. As a consequence the *Auraicept*, as the book which defines and articulates such a prodigious event, was considered to be an allegory of the world.

It is interesting to remark that a quasi-similar theory was expressed by a contemporary of Dante, I mean the great twelfth-century cabalist Abraham Abulafia. According to this very ingenious and perspicacious scholar, God gave Adam not a specific tongue but rather something like a model or a sort of method, a universal grammatical competence that, lost with the scandal of Babel, survived among the Jewish people who were so particularly skilled in the practice of that golden rule as to form the most perfect of the 70 post-babelic languages: the Hebrew tongue. And the Hebrew of which Abulafia spoke was not understood as a collage of other tongues, but rather as a brand new organism produced by the combination of the original 22 letters (the elementary and basically constitutive segments) of the divine alphabet: divine precisely because directly inspired by God himself.

Unlike Abulafia and others who pursued an approach similar to his, Irish grammarians did not decide to go back in time, in order to find, retrieve and restore a lost Adamic language, but decided rather to construct a totally new and quite original perfect tongue, to be identified with their own national idiom. Its invention did not demand the denial and deletion of the post-babelic experience, but rather its acceptance, with the laborious enterprise of reforming and reshaping the existing post-babelic languages.

And so we are faced with a problem. Did Joyce know this theory, embedded in his cultural tradition, about Irish as a perfect language? I have not found any reference to the *Auraicept* in the Joycean opus. However, my intellectual curiosity has been challenged and excited by the fact – reported by Richard Ellman – that the young bachelor, in October 1901, at the assembly of the Law Students' Debating Society, attended a lecture delivered by John F. Taylor. The speaker not only duly extolled the beauty and perfection of Irish, but also drew a parallel between the right of the Irish people to adopt and use this language, and the right that Moses and the Jewish nation had to use Hebrew as the language of divine revelation, refusing to adopt in captivity the Egyptian tongue imposed by their rulers. As we know,

Taylor's ideas were extensively recycled and intertextualised in the *Aeolus* chapter of *Ulysses*, which is centred on the parallelism between Hebrew and Irish. It will immediately be observed that this comparative parallelism comes to represent a sort of linguistic counterpart to the correspondence that links Bloom and Stephen.

Allow me, now, to entertain a suspicion or, if you prefer, to suggest a hypothesis. In *Finnegans Wake* (at page 356) we encounter the word *taylorised* that Atherton[4] interprets as a reference to Thomas Taylor, the neoplatonist. I am rather inclined to interpret it as a reference to John Taylor. To tell you the truth, I have no satisfactory and definitive evidence to sustain my hypothesis. However, it seems to me curious and interesting that such a word should be found in a context (*Finnegans Wake*, 353ff.) where Joyce writes of the *abnihilisation of the etym*, uses expressions such as *vociferagitant, viceversounding* and *alldconfusalem*, and ends with *how comes every a body in our taylorised world to selve out thisthis*, with a reference to the *primeum nobilees* and to the word *notomise*. Maybe Joyce's idea of inventing languages by dissecting and anatomising etyms was inspired by that lecture delivered by Taylor, in Jim's youth, together with some indirectly received concepts from the *Auraicept*. But since there is not textual evidence to fully warrant what I suspect to be the case, I can only offer my innuendo as a tempting hypothesis, or as a teasing idiosyncrasy.

There is no proof that Joyce was actually familiar with the early or late medieval Irish traditions. In his lecture *Ireland, Island of Saints and Sages,* given in Trieste in 1907, Joyce insisted on the antiquity or the ancient origins of the Irish language, and he went so far as to identify it with Phoenician. We know, of course, that Joyce was no historian, and – as it happens – in that lecture he even confused, as if they were the same person, John Scotus Eriugena (who was definitely an Irishman of the ninth century) with John Duns Scotus (born in Edinburgh in the thirteenth century, even though in Joyce's day many still believed he was Irish). In a similarly misguided fashion he believed that the author of the *Corpus Dionysianum,* whom he calls the pseudo-Areopagite Dionysius, was Saint Denis patron saint of the French nation. As we know, the Dionysius of the *Corpus* was identified by the medieval tradition with that Dionysius *Areopagite* who lived at the time of Saint Paul. However, that tradition-ally prevailing identification was also wrong. The real author of the *Corpus* was a pseudo-Dionysius Areopagite and, anyway, not a Dionysius pseudo-Areopagite, as Joyce claimed. But then, we must remember that, as an undergraduate at University College, Joyce studied Latin, French, English, Mathe-matics, Natural Philosophy and Logic, but never read Medieval Philosophy.

In any case, all the analogies to be found between the claims of the Medieval Irish grammarians and the Joycean quest for a perfect poetic language are so striking that I shall pursue the search of other probable connections.

The Book of Kells

In order to design his own poetic language Joyce, even though feebly equipped with very approximate and imprecise ideas about Medieval scholarship and armed with a shaky knowledge of the old Irish tradition, could make reference to a text which he knew rather well and which he quoted explicitly, for the first time, in his Trieste lecture on Ireland. I mean, of course, the *Book of Kells*.

Joyce as a young man had presumably seen the *Book* at Trinity College, and later he referred to a reproduction, more precisely to *The Book of Kells, described by Sir Edward Sullivan, and illustrated with twenty-four plates in colour* (2nd ed., London, Paris, New York, 1920), even though, in his last years, as his eyesight worsened, he could only make references to the *Book* from memory. (Incidentally, Joyce presented a copy of this reproduction to Miss Weaver, as a Christmas gift, in 1922).

Recently, in my Introduction to the marvellous facsimile of the manuscript of Trinity College Library,[5] I suggested that this masterpiece of Irish art was preceded and surrounded by a 'murmur' and I am sure that, even if only in an indirect way, Joyce was influenced by that mysterious and beckoning murmur. Two days ago I spent an afternoon (for the second time in my life) in what I consider the most magic place in Ireland: the monastic site of the old abbey of Clonmacnoise and its seven churches, and once again I realised that nobody, even without knowledge of the Irish grammarians, or of the Books *of Kells, Durrow, Lindisfarne* or *Dun Cow,* could possibly gaze at that landscape and at those old stones without sensing, at once, the captivating murmur that accompanied the birth and the millenary life of the *Book of Kells.*

The historical accounts of Latin culture, before the year 1000 and particularly between the seventh and the tenth centuries, register the development of that which has been called 'Hisperic aesthetics': a style and a sensibility that emerged in Spain and, in its evolution, migrated to the British Isles, touching Gaul as well. The classic Latin tradition had already described (and condemned) that kind of style, characterising it as 'Asian', and then as 'African', considering it as alien and opposed to the equilibrium of the 'Attic' style. Quintilian, in his *Institutio oratoria* (XII, 79), had already stressed that the perfect style must impart '*magna non nimia* (grandeur, not superfluity), *sublimia non abrupta* (the sublime, not the abrupt), *fortia non temeraria* (strength, not temerity), *severa non tristia* (severity, not gloom), *gravia non tarda* (substance, not dullness), *laeta non luxuriosa* (happiness, not extravagance), *iucunda non dissoluta* (joy, not laxity), *grandia non tumida* (greatness, not turgidity)'. Not only the Roman but also the early Christian rhetoric condemned the *Kakozelon* or bad affectation of the 'Asian' style, and as an example of how greatly scandalised were the Church Fathers when confronted with examples of this *mala affectatio,* consider St Jerome's invective:

> There are by now so many barbaric writers and so many discourses rendered confusing through vices of style, that we have reached a point where one can no longer comprehend either who is speaking or what is being discussed. Everything [in such writings] is inflated and then collapses like a sick snake that breaks itself up into bits while trying its contortions. . . . Everything is twisted into inextricable verbal knots and one should echo, with Plautus: 'Here, no one – except the Sibyl – can understand anything.' But what use has such-like witchcraft of words? (*Adversus Jovinianum* I)

A spiteful description, by a nostalgic traditionalist, of a page from the *Book of Kells* or from *Finnegans Wake,* would sound not unlike St Jerome's tirade. But regardless of St Jerome's rhetorical preferences, inevitably something was to happen: those qualities which, according to Classical tradition, were classified as 'vices', in Hisperic poetics became virtues.

The Hisperic page no longer obeyed the laws of traditional syntax and rhetoric. The norms of rhythm and of metre were violated in order to produce elements imbued with what we would call a Baroque flavour. Extended chains of alliterations that the Classic world would have considered cacophonous began to produce a new music, while Aldhelm of Malmesbury delighted in constructing sentences in which each word begins with the same letter, for instance: 'Primitus pantorum procerum praetorumque pio potissimum, paternoque praesertim privilegio panegyricum poemataque passim prosatori sub polo promulgantes. . .'.[6]

The Hisperic lexicon became enriched with numerous, quite extraordinary and most unexpected hybrids, by borrowing Hebrew terms as well as Hellenisms, while the discourse became heavily burdened with cryptograms and riddles that defy any attempt at translation. If Classical aesthetics had clarity as its ideal, Hisperic aesthetics pursued obscurity. If Classical aesthetics exalted proportion, Hisperic aesthetics privileged and exploited complexity, the abundance of epithets and periphrases, the gigantic, the monstrous, the uncontainable, the immeasurable, the prodigious. The same search for unacceptable etymologies led to the dissection of words into atomistic elements that inevitably acquired enigmatic meanings.

Hisperic aesthetics came to represent the sensibility and the style of a Europe living its Dark Ages during which the old continent suffered a decline in population, a crisis in agricultural skills, the destruction of its great cities, of its roads, of the Roman aqueducts. In a vast landscape largely consisting of neglected woodland, not only monks, but also poets and miniaturists were to view the world as a dark, forbidding forest teeming with monsters, crisscrossed by labyrinthine pathways. In these difficult and disorderly centuries, it was from Ireland that the Latin culture was brought back to the continent. However, those Irish monks, who had preserved and elaborated for us that small amount of the Classic heritage which they had managed to save, moved within the world of language and of visual imagination as if groping their way through thick and dark woods. Or, otherwise, we could imagine them as companions of St Brendan, tossed about at sea, encountering monsters and uncharted islands, and a gigantic fish upon which they would disembark, mistaking it for an island, and the island of white birds (which are those souls who had fallen with Lucifer), and miraculous fountains and trees from Paradise, and a column made of crystal in the middle of the sea, and Judas, prisoner upon a rock, beaten and tormented by the ceaseless waves.

Between the seventh and ninth centuries, perhaps on Irish soil (but certainly in the British Isles), there appeared that *Liber monstrorum de diversis generibus* that seems to describe so many of the images we encounter again in the *Book of Kells*. Its author confesses in the opening pages that, although so many authoritative books had already recounted such falsehoods, he would have never considered propounding them again if 'the impetuous wind of your request had not arrived unexpectedly and cast me – such a fearful sailor – headlong into a sea of monsters'. The nature of this sea is revealed at the beginning of the second book:

> Infinite, without any doubt, are the species of wild marine creatures, with bodies as enormous as high mountains, that violently stir up with their chests the most gigantic waves and vast expanses of water, almost extirpating them from the depths, as they move toward the gentle outlets of the rivers; swimming, they produce foam and spray, with great noise. . . . Overturning with a horrible undertow those waters already churned by the great masses and movements of their bodies, they head straight for shore, presenting a terrifying spectacle to those who gaze upon them.

However fearful the author may be of telling lies, he cannot resist the abysmal beauty of this fascinating untruth, because it allows him to weave a tale as infinite and varied as a labyrinth. He tells his tale with the same relish with which, in the *Vita S. Columbani,* the sea around the island of Hibernia is described; or, as in the *Hisperica famina* (a work with which the author of the

Liber monstrorum may have been familiar), such adjectives as *astriferus* or *glaucicomus* are used to describe the waves of the sea. Hisperian aesthetics would have also appreciated neologisms such as *pectoreus, placoreus, sonoreus, alboreus, propriferus, flamminger,* and *gaudifluus.*

These are the same lexical inventions praised by Virgilius Grammaticus in his *Epitomae* and in his *Epistulae.* Many scholars now maintain that this insane grammarian of Bigorre, a region near Toulouse, was in reality an Irishman. And, to my mind, everything – from his prose style to his vision of the world – would tend to confirm this hypothesis.

Virgilius lived in the seventh century and, therefore, presumably one hundred years before the *Book of Kells* was produced. He 'quoted' passages from Cicero or Virgil (the other, the true prototypical Virgil!), which those authors could not possibly have written. And then we discover that he belonged to a clique of rhetoricians who shared a common inclination: the adoption of the names of Classical authors as their own. Virgilius, in reality, was citing the inventions of his own friends. Perhaps he invented them. Perhaps, as has been conjectured, he wrote in that fashion in order to poke fun at other (traditional) rhetoricians. Influenced by Celtic, Visigothic, Irish, and Hebrew cultures, he presented an uncanny linguistic universe that seems to have erupted from the imagination of a modern surrealist poet.

He argues that there are twelve varieties of Latin and that, in each, the word for fire can be a different term, such as *ignis, quoquihabin, ardon, calax, spiridon, rusin, fragon, fumaton, ustrax, vitius, siluleus, aeneon* (*Epitomae* I, 4). A battle is called *praelium* because it takes place at sea – called *praelum* because its vastness bears the primacy, or *praelatum,* of the marvellous (*Epitomae* IV, 10). Geometry is an art that expounds upon all the experiments with herbs and plants, and that is why physicians are called geometricians (*Epitomae* IV, 11). The rhetorician Aemilius elegantly proclaimed SSSSSSSSSS. PP. NNNNNNNN. GGGG.R.MM.TTT.D. CC. AAAAAAA. IIIII. VVVVVVVV. O. AE. EEEEEEE. – which should mean 'the wise man sucks the blood of wisdom and must appropriately be called a leech of the veins' (*Epitomae* X, I). Galbungus and Terrentius engaged for fourteen days and fourteen nights in a debate concerning the vocative case of *ego,* and the problem was seen as of the utmost importance because it concerns the question of determining how one may emphatically address oneself ('Oh, I, have I done well?' *O egone, recte feci?*). This, and more, Virgilius tells us, and he makes us think of the young Joyce who asked if baptism by mineral water should be deemed as valid.

Each of the texts I have mentioned could be used to describe a page of the *Book of Kells,* as well as a page of *Finnegans Wake,* because in each one the language behaves just as the images unfold in the *Book*. To use words for the purpose of describing the *Book of Kells* means to re-invent a page of Hisperic literature. The *Book* is a luscious vegetation of interlace, of stylised animal forms, of small simian figures amidst impossible foliage that covers page after page, as if in pursuit of motifs (always the same ones) of a tapestry, whereas – in reality – each line, each corymb, represents a different invention. It is a complication of spiral-shaped turns intentionally ignorant of any educated norm of symmetry. It is, at once, a symphony of delicate or vibrant colours, from pink to yellow orange, from lemon yellow to purplish red. Quadrupeds, birds, greyhounds sporting the beak of a swan, unthinkable humanoid figures contorted like a circus acrobat with his head between his knees, while twisting the head to form an initial letter; nimble beings as flexible as coloured rubber bands introduce themselves into the entanglement of the enlacements, poke their heads through the abstract decorations, entwine themselves around those initials, insinuate themselves between the lines. The page quivers restlessly under our gaze; it seems animated by a life of its own. There are no points of precise reference, everything is mingled with everything else. The *Book of Kells* is the kingdom of Proteus. It is the product of a cold-blooded hallucination that did not require any mescaline or lysergic acid to produce these abysmal labyrinths, also because it does not represent the delirium of a single mind, but rather the delirium of an entire culture engaged in a dialogue with itself and citing other Gospels, other illuminated letters, other tales.

The *Book* is the lucid vertigo of a language that is trying to redefine the world while redefining itself, with the full realisation that – in a dark and uncertain age – the key to the revelation of the world is not to be found in a straight line but rather within the labyrinth. And it was, therefore, not by chance that it inspired *Finnegans Wake*, where Joyce endeavoured to produce a book that would constitute, at once, an image of the universe and a work intended for an 'ideal reader affected by an ideal insomnia'.

But even in relation to *Ulysses*, Joyce had already stated that many of the initials in the *Book of Kells* possessed the quality of an entire chapter in his book, and explicitly asked that his entire work be compared to those miniatures.

The particular chapter in *Finnegans Wake* that makes specific reference to the *Book of Kells* is the one conventionally called *The Manifesto of Alp*. In this chapter is narrated the story of a letter that is found on a manure heap, in 'a midden'. That letter is a symbol for the inhabited world in which men have left so many traces. It stands as a symbol for all attempts at written communication including all other letters, the total universe of literature, the *Book of Kells*, all manuscripts, all the sacred books of the world, and also *Finnegans Wake* itself. The page in the *Book of Kells* in which Joyce found his most powerful source of inspiration is the 'tenebrous Tunc' page (folio 124r).

If one allows one's eye to casually travel over the 'Tunc' page while simultaneously reading, even if in a random skipping fashion, some of Joyce's lines, the impression one has is that of a mixed-media experience, in which the language mirrors the images of the illuminations, and the images of the illuminations stimulate and engender linguistic analogies.

Joyce explicitly refers to a page where 'every person, place and thing in the chaosmos of Alle amyway connected with the gobblydumped turkey was moving and changing every part of the time'. He speaks of a 'steady monologue of interiors' where 'a word as cunningly hidden in its maze of confused drapery as a fieldmouse in a nest of coloured ribbons' becomes an 'Ostrogothic kakography affected for certain phrases of Etruscan stable-talk' made of 'utterly unexpected sinistrogyric return to one peculiar sore point in the past . . . indicating that the words which follow may be taken in any order desired. . . .'.

What is it that more precisely and fully reveals the presence of the *Book of Kells* in the pages of *Finnegans Wake*? Here you have it:

. . . those haughtypitched disdotted aiches easily of the
rariest inasdroll as most of the jaywalking eyes we do plough
into halve, unconnected, principial, medial or final, always
jims in the jam, sahib, as pipless as threadworms: the
innocent exhibitionism of those frank yet capricious under-
linings: that strange exotic serpentine, since so properly
banished from our scripture, about as freakwing a wetter-
hand now as to see a rightheaded ladywhite don a cork-
horse, which, in its invincible insolence ever longer more
and of more morosity, seems to uncoil spirally and
swell lacertinelazily before our eyes under pressure of the
writer's hand; . . . then (coming over to the left aisle
corner down) the cruciform postscript from which three
basia or shorter and smaller *oscula* have been overcare-
fully scraped away, plainly inspiring the tenebrous *Tunc*
page of the Book of Kells. . . .[7]

Thus it is that this ancient manuscript speaks of
something that we can recognise. It speaks of a world
made of pathways that branch in opposite directions,
about adventures of the mind and of the imagination that
cannot be narrated. It is a structure where every point can
be connected to every other, where there are no points or
positions but only lines of connection, any one of which
may be interrupted at any stage whatsoever since it
will begin immediately to follow the same line. It can
be disconnected and overturned, it has not centre nor
periphery. The *Book of Kells* is a perfect labyrinth. That is
why it could stand, to the excited mind of Joyce, as the

model of an infinite book still to be written, readable only by an ideal reader affected by an ideal insomnia.

But at the same time the *Book of Kells* (along with its remote offspring, *Finnegans Wake*) represents the model of human language and, perhaps, of the world we live in. Perhaps we are living inside a Book not unlike the *Book of Kells*, while believing to live inside Diderot's *Encyclopedia*. Both the *Book of Kells* and *Finnegans Wake* constitute the most powerful images of the universe in expansion, perhaps finite but still unlimited, and the starting point of infinite interrogations. These two uncanny and disconcerting documents allow us to take cognisance of ourselves as men and women of our own time, even as we navigate across the same perilous sea that carried St Brendan in his search of the Lost Island that the *Book* celebrates on every page, while inviting and inspiring us to pursue our quest for a perfect way to express the imperfect world we live in.

Bachelor Jim was far from unaccomplished, for he foresaw, as through a foggy mist, what he had to do and what we have to understand, namely, that linguistic ambiguity, the natural imperfection of our idioms, is not a post-babelic disease from which mankind should recover, but is rather the only chance that God gave Adam, the speaking animal. To understand that human languages are open, imperfect and capable of begetting that supreme imperfection that we call poetry, constitutes the only aim of any quest for perfection. Babel was not an accident. We have been living in the Tower from the beginning. The first dialogue between God and Adam took place in Finneganian labyrinths, and only by returning to Babel and accepting the only real chance available to us, can we find our peace and embrace the limits, the vocation and the destiny of our human condition.

The whole story started in Dublin, when a young man began to be haunted by the images of the books of Kells, of Durrow, of Dun Cow. 'Once upon a time there was a Dun Cow coming down along the maze and this Dun Cow book that was coming down along the maze met a nicens little boy named baby Jim the bachelor. . .'.

Notes

1. The lecture mentioned in *Stephen Hero* is a different one, based on the text of the later lecture, of 1902, on Mangan.
2. *The Critical Writings of James Joyce.* Ellsworth Mason and Richard Ellman (eds). London: Faber & Faber, and New York: Viking, 1959, p. 45. I shall refer to this work in the text as (*CW*, page number).
3. I am referring to the beautiful study by Diego Poli: 'La metafora di Babele e le *partitiones* nella teoria grammaticale irlandese dell'*Auraicept na n-Éces*', in D. Poli, ed., *Episteme, Quaderni Linguistici e Filologici*, IV, 1986–1989. Università di Macerata, Istituto di Glottologia e Linguistica generale, pp. 179–98.

4. James Atherton *The Books of the Wake: A Study of Literary Allusions in James Joyce's* Finnegans Wake. London: Faber & Faber, 1959; New York: Viking, 1960

5. *The Book of Kells (Ms 58, Trinity College Library Dublin).* Commentary edited by Peter Fox. Fine Art Facsimile Publishers of Switzerland. Luzern: Faksimile Verlag, 1990.

6. *Epistola III Aldhelmi ad Eahfridum ex Hibernia in patriam reversum*, in *PL*, Vol. 89, p. 91.

7. James Joyce, *Finnegans Wake*. London: Faber & Faber, 1939, pp. 121–2. Quotation © Copyright the Estate of James Joyce.

Joyce's Dialogue with Aquinas, Dante, Bruno, Vico, Svevo . . .

Liberato Santoro-Brienza

Joyce and Italy

Much could be said, and indeed much has already been written, about James Joyce's sojourns in Italy and about his experiences among my people. Even more could be said about the 'influence' on Joyce of Italian writers and thinkers. I shall talk mainly about this second theme, with particular reference to selected encounters or dialogues between our Dublin hero and some Italian literary and philosophical figures towards whom he felt proximity, empathy and congeniality.

Joyce's existential, spiritual and literary connections with the Italian people and culture are numerous, deep and substantial. Quite significantly, to mention a fact often underestimated if not completely overlooked, the Italian language and the distinct Triestine vernacular were adopted as, we might say, the official languages of the Joyce family. The dialect of Trieste remained their household tongue, long after their departure from Italy.

Landed in Trieste at the precocious age of twenty-two, Joyce was to produce most – if not all – of his monumental work under Italian skies and in dialogue with the Italian spirits he had adopted as his artistic mentors. Jim's arrival in Italy – regardless of his young age – was not premature. The butterfly was already well-shaped inside the cocoon. It had already acquired the foretaste of infinite space, as the artist had already made his clear connections with the universal destiny of Western literature. Aquinas, Dante, Bruno, Vico (with Shakespeare and later with Homer whom he came to frequent through Francis Bacon's reading of Greek mythology) had been the channels of his inward meta-morphosis and the heavenly bridges to connect the Dublin-Ireland microcosm with the macrocosm of universal culture. Joyce was proud of his chosen mentors and proud of his choice. And we sense a warm touch of filial gratitude in his numerous references to Aquinas, Bruno, Vico and – more so – Dante Alighieri. Equally sensitive, though perhaps less touching and certainly less dramatic, are his expressions of recognition towards Italo Svevo. By adopting this disposition, Joyce was also cele-brating Dante – especially – who never failed to acknowl-edge his gratitude towards his own guide and counsellor, Virgil. Finally, on this point, through the indirect media-tion of Samuel Beckett's essay entitled *Dante. . . . Bruno. Vico. . Joyce,*[1] which the author undertook to write after

Joyce's explicit suggestion and under his constant super-
vision, Joyce paid his penultimate instalment of debt to
his main spiritual guides and mentors.

In his early years in Trieste, and then especially in
Rome, James Joyce did not behave like a character that
we would call *simpatico*. We know that he systematically
failed – among others – to pay the rent for his accom-
modation: a practice that inevitably led to his migrating
from flat to flat; or failed to meet the deadlines of his
frequent debts. We also know, from his pen, the general
dislike he felt towards Rome and the Romans, in particular. And I am inclined to find Richard Ellmann's
account of Joyce's Roman misbehaviour, both apologetic
and perhaps too generously tolerant, when he writes:

> He naturally vented some of his irritation on the Italians.
> Every letter reported some new cause of fury. In August he
> determined that Rome, unlike Trieste, had not one decent
> café. In September an official refused to cash a telegraphic
> money order from Stanislaus because Joyce did not have
> his passport with him. Joyce cried in rage, 'By Jesus, Rossini
> was right when he took off his hat to the Spaniard, saying
> 'You save me from the shame of being the last in Europe.'
> 'The quotation did not win the official over. . . . But
> most of Joyce's anger was born of impatience, as when on
> December 3 he declared the 'chief pastime and joke' of
> Henry James's 'subtle Romans' to be 'the breaking of wind
> rereward. . . . However, it is an expletive which I am
> reserving for the day when I leave the eternal city as my

farewell and adieu to it.' . . . Four days later he remarked, 'I am damnably sick of Italy, Italian and the Italians, outrageously, illogically sick.' He went on grudgingly, 'I hate to think that Italians ever did anything in the way of art. But I suppose they did.' Then, as if he had conceded too much, he wrote in the margin, 'What did they do but illustrate a page or so of the New Testament!' He was weary of their '*bello*' and '*bellezza*', and carried on his irritation to *Ulysses*, where Bloom, on hearing some cab-men talk Italian, comments on their 'beautiful language' and '*Bella Poetria*', only to be assured by Stephen that they were haggling obscenely over money.[2]

I shall refrain from mentioning even less flattering and more disgusting comments made by Joyce as a young bank clerk in the eternal city. It seems clear, anyway, that all too often Joyce the man was downright *antipatico*. Fortunately, his talent for perspicacious observation and his wit have given us some funny remarks. For instance, he amusingly commented on the names of some fellow-clerks (which, by the way, he clearly didn't find 'offensive' as Ellmann erroneously maintains). 'A clerk here is named (he is round, bald, fat, voiceless) Bartoluzzi. You pronounce by inflating both cheeks and prolonging the u. Every time I pass him I repeat his name to myself and translate "Good day, little bits of Barto." Another is named Simonetti'. – Joyce concluded: 'They are all little bits of something or other, I think' (Ellmann, 226).[3]

I also find amusing, though cruelly apposite and in the vein of black humour, his comment of 25 September, 1906, when – after a sightseeing expedition to the ancient Roman forum – he remarked: 'Rome reminds me of a man who lives by exhibiting to travellers his grandmother's corpse'. (Ellmann, 225)[4] The fact that Rome was a rather small and, in many respects, an intellectually provincial and peripheral city; Joyce's frustrated expectations of the city and of his new job in the Bank, which – I believe – he undertook mainly in the hope that it would gain him access to more affluent and sophisticated social circles; his relative lack of creativity and literary productivity; all these reasons do not hide the fact that, in Rome, Joyce was – as I have said – *antipatico*, at his best perhaps. We must however be cautious, for we know almost nothing of his carefree disposition when in the copious company of white wine. In fact, we can surmise and should not doubt that – especially on those occasions – Jim must have been, more than charming and amusing, the heart and soul of the party. Aware of his talented voice, personally I have no difficulty in imagining Jim ready to gratify his fellow-drinkers with a few well-tuned tunes.

What really matters in the end, as Thomas Aquinas has suggested, is not the artist's personal disposition, passions, idiosyncrasies, ethical inclinations and temperament, but only the quality of his work. And we must acknowledge that Joyce was at work, attending to his appointed task, even when all he seemed to do was to indulge his calculated arrogance and his apparent insensitive selfishness. We know that for Joyce – perhaps more than for any other writer in the universal history of literature – everything that he could observe and everything that he could experience was grist to his creative mill. In this he is, to us, what Homer was to Greek culture, what Dante was to the Medieval and Renaissance world, what Shakespeare represented for the dawn of modern Britain, what Goethe signified for the incipient German national consciousness.

In voluntary exile, the Italian experience did Jim no harm! I mean that precisely his at times jaundiced, always very personal and original perception of the human world, also as he observed it among the much criticised Romans, became eventually material for his epic treatment of the human substance: without idealisation, with almost dispassionate distant gaze.

Exile was for Jim the opportune time and condition for verifying and working out for himself the role of the artist, just as he formulated it in the pages of *A Portrait* (219):

> The personality of the artist, at first a cry or a cadence or a mood and then a fluid and lambent narrative, finally refines itself out of existence, impersonalises itself, so to speak.

The aesthetic image in the dramatic form is life purified in and reprojected from the human imagination. The mystery of aesthetic like that of material creation is accomplished. The artist, like the God of the creation, remains within or behind or beyond or above his handiwork, invisible, refined out of existence, indifferent, paring his fingernails.

It is worth noting Lynch's response to Stephen's poetic manifesto:

– What do you mean, Lynch asked surlily, by prating about beauty and the imagination in this miserable Godforsaken island? No wonder the artist retired within or behind his handiwork after having perpetrated this country.

The reality of experience and of observation pervades his often cruelly realistic re-creation, through literature, of human life. I would venture to say that the existential exposure to the often crazy, operatic and heroic-comic ways of the Italians nourished Joyce's growth from his inner world of adolescent autobiographical introspection: I mean, from the real/imaginary Irish world of *Dubliners, Stephen Hero* and – to a certain extent – *A Portrait,* to the open universe of *Ulysses* and *Finnegans Wake.*

The writer has recorded a veritable encyclopedia of insights into the no matter how small and apparently insignificant habits, quirks and mannerisms of the

Italians, as he saw them. And I strongly believe there is still at least a good book to be written on this subject. In particular, Joyce was keen to record – especially in *Ulysses* – things to do with bodily cleanliness (or the lack thereof), the preoccupation with bodily organs and functions, ways of practising sexual intercourse. His final narratives can be read as in-between humour and shock, playfulness and perversion. I am sure that even in this – in his perception (whether real or imaginary) of other ways of living, eating, being aware of one's bodily organs and expressing or deploying one's body – the Italian experience did Jim-the-writer no harm.

As Umberto Eco has reminded us, an article in a 1901 issue of *St Stephen's* accusingly criticised Jim, then in his years at University College, for having been corrupted by Italian influences. I am sure that, despite his official canonisation (which, I suspect, he would have rather declined), it was not Thomas Aquinas who was held responsible for young Jim's intellectual and spiritual corruption. Presumably also Dante – with whom Joyce conversed in his studies – could hardly have been seen as a corrupting influence, at the time. But then, who knows?, considering that the divine poet never missed a chance of sternly chastising misbehaving priests, prelates, bishops and popes, with a passion for truth and justice which he would – when dealing with unassuming mortals – temper and soften with tolerance and compassion.[5]

The suspicion of the Italian corrupting influence on the young Joyce must surely refer to Jim's – as a young Italianist – interest in D'Annunzio and his sympathy towards Giordano Bruno. In those early years, Jim the student identified with D'Annunzio's heroic ideals of the aesthetic life, not unlike Ibsen's and the Symbolists' search for a synthesis of life and art, and with Bruno's rebellious disposition towards any form of temporal authority and dogmatic power: whether Church or State. With reference to D'Annunzio, it has been noted that Joyce had studied him 'so closely that he could imitate his manner', (Ellmann, 59), to the point of baffling the examiners of his last Italian test-paper at College. He admired the musical diction of D'Annunzio's writings. And we cannot fail to remark on the similar quality of Joyce's prose that yields a lyrical poetical subtle musicality. (Ah, if Yeats had only been endowed with a little more of Joyce's musical sensibility. . .!).

With regard to Giordano Bruno, in whose honour a statue had been erected – in 1889 – in Campo dei Fiori (where he had been burned at the stake in the year 1600), to vindicate the merit and distinction of this great philosopher, Joyce's sympathy must have been well known in College. I think it is significant that the name of Bruno the Nolan is mentioned in one of the final pages of *A Portrait*:

24 March: . . . Then went to college. Other wrangle with little roundhead rogue'seye Ghezzi. This time about Bruno the Nolan. Began in Italian and ended in pidgin English. He said Bruno was a terrible heretic. I said he was terribly burned. He agreed to this with some sorrow. Then gave me recipe for what he calls *risotto alla bergamasca*. (*A Portrait*, 253)

In the final dialogues between Stephen and his sweetheart, Joyce does not hide pertinent clues as traits that identify him with Giordano Bruno. The girl speaks first:

– You are a great stranger now.
– Yes. I was born to be a monk.
– I am afraid you are a heretic. (*A Portrait*, 224)

At this point Stephen has already taken flight from the spiritual paralysis of his country. The butterfly is beating, with restless fluttering wings, at its cocoon. Dedalus, the prototypical artist, is fully formed, wearing also the intellectual garb and disguise of the heretic monk.

Years later, especially in the writing of *Ulysses* and *Finnegans Wake*, Joyce was to treasure and apply, in his poetic strategies, Bruno's idea of a final cosmic unification, as an identity of contraries or – in Cusanus's formula – as the ultimate *coincidentia oppositorum*, of all the temporal oppositions and divisions that make up the chaos of lived experience. In *Finnegans Wake*, in particular, Joyce was to symbolise in the personification of Shem and Shaun the fundamental oppositions of the chaotic world in which he lived and of the conflicting tendencies within his own personal history and his poetic universe. In the same work he also granted Bruno of Nola an Irish identity, by intentionally confusing him with the Dublin booksellers, *Browne and Nolan.*

The Italian experience and even the Roman sojourn did young Jim-the-writer no harm! He may have been restless and frustrated, he may have been drinking a little too much white wine – and that did him no good! – he may have been deluded in his expectations of social recognition, during the months he spent in the eternal city. And yet, in his customary manner which is also a mark of his genius, he managed to get something out of it. The city – regardless of all her failings and idiosyncrasies – bearing the marks of her ancient glory, still proudly announces her ancestral role as *umbilicus terrae*, sacred place, omphalos and navel of the earth. The lure of this 'great mother's corpse' did not leave Joyce untouched. More so, I am convinced that Rome's 'eternal' identity, her ability to adapt and survive, her troubled history, her dramatic vicissitudes, the ancient tokens of her epic and heroic past, that place her almost above time or, otherwise, that make her encompass time; all this must have streghtened, if not triggered, in the mind of James Joyce the vision of a universal history of human experience: beyond time while within time – albeit, time at once inflated and collapsed. I think it was in Rome, the city immersed in memory and stage of heroic-comic spectacles, it was in Rome that Joyce began to see everyday human experience – no matter how banal and insignificant – *sub specie aeternitatis*; just as he had learnt, in Dublin, to read the wisdom of Aquinas *sub specie temporis nostri*.

Two fragments of his correspondence from Rome bear witness to an incipient new plan. On 30 September 1906, Jim appended a P.P.S. to a postcard addressed to Stanislaus,[6] where he mentioned the idea of writing an additional story for *Dubliners*, to be entitled *Ulysses* and dealing with the plight and vicissitudes of the Dubliner Mr Hunter. The idea remained firm in his mind. So that, on 13 November, in a letter to his brother, Jim mentioned that he had not started work on the planned new story. But he added, with an obvious sense of excitement: 'Do you like the title of my story about Hunter?'. Alfred H. Hunter was a mild and undistinguished character in the Dublin microcosm familiar to Joyce who had met him only on few occasions. It was said of him that he was a Jew and that his wife betrayed him. A story also has it that, in 1904, Mr Hunter, like the good Samaritan, did Joyce a good turn by helping him, drunk, out of a brawl, and by taking him back to his home. In this incident is to be found the factual prototype of the 15th episode of *Ulysses*, where Bloom comes to Stephen's rescue and takes him back to his flat.

The picture or vision of the humiliated, alienated and cuckolded Jew gained strength in his mind, with the reading of Ferrero's critical attacks on anti-Semitic theories. Joyce began to see also the connections between the wandering Jew and both Homer's and Dante's wandering Ulysses. Most importantly, for his subsequent writing of *Ulysses* and *Finnegans Wake,* he saw the connection between Ulysses/the Jew and himself as the exile. For the same connection, he also formed in his mind a closer affinity with Italo Svevo.

It was in Rome that Joyce fully lived the experience of estrangement and alienation that belongs to the emigrant and exile. His self-imposed exile may have been, at first, only an imaginary act of intellectual distancing, an affirmation of spiritual independence, a literary device for the purpose of forging his own personal and artistic identity, perhaps even an aesthetic experiment at emulating the divine poet Dante. In 1906, in Rome, life caught up with his art, experience rushed into his literature, hardship and suffering filled his intentions. In that same year, Joyce must have savoured fully the meaning of Dante's lines, where the poet makes his ancestor Cacciaguida warn him:

Tu lascerai ogni cosa diletta
Più caramente, e questo è quello strale
Che l'arco dell'esilio pria saetta

Tu proverai sì come sa di sale
　Lo pane altrui, e com' è duro calle
　Lo scendere e il salir per l'altrui scale.

[You shall leave everything beloved most dearly; and this is the arrow which the bow of exile shoots first. You shall come to know how salt is the taste of another's bread, and how hard the path to climb and to descend by others' stairs.][7]

Dante

I have often returned to Via Frattina (just around the corner from where Shelley, Byron and Keats had once lived) and I have stopped at No. 52, to read the marble plaque placed there, in 1982, to celebrate the centenary of Joyce's birth. I have looked up at the wall above the doorway and read the touching and dramatic words 'esule volontario'. In Joyce's 'voluntary exile' we find the first connection with Dante. It is a connection, but it is also a *coincidentia oppositorum*. Dante's exile was involuntary and imposed. Furthermore, unlike Dante, Joyce did not have to face death, had he returned to Dublin. Dante's penalty, on the contrary, was death by burning, had he ever returned to Florence. In 1303, the year after his condemnation to exile and death, the penalty of exile was extended also to his children, upon completion of their fourteenth birthday. In 1315 – twelve years later! – after his renewed refusal to plead guilty, Dante was again condemned to death. This time the penalty was extended also to his sons. The savagely extreme and unwarranted severity of the imposed penalties indicates the virulence of political passions in Dante's Florence and in the papal Rome. In his *Commedia*, the poet never missed a chance to chastise those who sinned through greed, envy, avarice, ambition and betrayal. In fact, only towards these did Dante show no compassion. Of course, we appreciate that – for Joyce, as he perceived it – Dublin and Ireland might have ministered another kind of death penalty: not physical death by burning, but spiritual extinction by political, religious, intellectual and artistic stagnation or repression. In exile, Jim the artist 'had retired within or behind or beyond or above his handiwork'.

In his condition of exile, Joyce shared another common trait with Dante Alighieri: they both held an ambiguous disposition towards their respective cities of origin; a contrasting sentiment, another *coincidentia oppositorum* of love and hate, nostalgia and rejection, the desire to belong and the need to keep distance.

In her tribute to Joyce, after his death, Elizabeth Bowen noted that there is less pity and less compassion in the writer's later works, and suggested that Joyce progressively distanced himself from pity and compassion, just as he progressively distanced himself from

Ireland and Dublin. Bowen suggested that he rejected
Ireland, tired of too much compassion; he went into
voluntary exile to forget his motherland. And yet,
Ireland and Dublin are to be felt ubiquitously present in
all his writings, as the concealed protagonists of his
poetic universe. Not unlike Florence for Dante, Dublin
works as an obsessional presence for Joyce. The scandal
of Parnell and the ensuing state of political, moral and
religious confusion, acted upon the young Jim as a deeply
felt trauma: they induced in him a sense of profound
mistrust in humanity and triggered his subsequent
rebellious and polemical anti-nationalism, anti-clericalism
and anti-Catholicism. Among other critics, Mario Praz
– also echoing J. Paris and P. Hutchins – has observed
that Dublin became for the artist, in *Dubliners* and in *A
Portrait*, a mirror of human foolishness – a ship-of-fools
– and of human decay. Joyce's attempts at suspending
time, in his later works, by deconstructing chronological
linearity, have also been interpreted as the desire to
locate his work and art beyond the reach of quotidian
pain and injury. He tried to abolish history, by inflating
beyond any conceivable boundary the span of a day, in
Ulysses, and the length of a night, in *Finnegans Wake*.[8]

Regardless of his efforts, even after the dissolution of
space and time, of linearity and determinism, causality
and traditional form, Joyce could not abandon his reference and anchorage to a place, the place, Dublin. It has

been said that if there were no extant physical traces of Dublin, one could reconstruct the city as it was for Joyce, from his innumerable and precise allusions and descriptions. As Florence for Dante and as Rome for the Romans, Dublin becomes – in the writings of her distinguished son – the omphalos, the *umbilicus mundi*. Dublin, the metropolis and microcosm of *Dubliners*, becomes a prison and labyrinth in *A Portrait*, metamorphoses into a metaphor of the Mediterranean sea in *Ulysses*, and finally expands and explodes to form a massive nebula and a galactic constellation in *Finnegans Wake*. Like Dante and like passionate betrayed lovers, 'Joyce hated and cursed, and at once idolised, his unfaithful object of love'.[9]

Dante's repeated attacks, criticisms, condemnations and curses addressed to Florence find an extremely passionate expression in one particular place of *Inferno* (XV: 61–9):

> Ma quell'ingrato populo maligno,
>> Che discese di Fiesole ab antico,
>> E tiene ancor del monte e del macigno,
> Ti si farà per tuo ben far, nimico:
>> Ed è ragion; chè tra li lazzi sorbi
>> Si disconvien fruttare al dolce fico.
> Vecchia fama nel mondo li chiama orbi;
>> Gente avara, invidiosa e superba,
>> Da' lor costumi fa che tu ti forbi.

[But that ungrateful and malignant race,
    Who in old times came down from Fiesole,
    Ay and still smack of their rough mountain-flint,
Will for thy good deeds show thee enmity.
    No wonder; for amongst ill-savour'd crabs
    It suits not the sweet fig-tree lay her fruit.
Old fame reports them in the world for blind,
    Covetous, envious, proud. Look to it well:
    Take heed thou cleanse thee of their ways.[10]]

At the same time, Dante could affectionately and touchingly refer to his native city as *il bell'ovile ov'io dormii agnello* [the fair sheepfold where slept I as a lamb] (*Paradiso* XXV: 5).

Although Joyce is generally less direct in his indictments against Dublin and Ireland, his voice truly acquires a Dantesque tone when, with acrimonious scorn, he calls Ireland 'the old sow that eats her farrow'. The entire conversation between Stephen and Davin reverberates with references to Dante, while summing-up Joyce's predicament and his need to escape.

– No honourable and sincere man, said Stephen, has given up to you his life and his youth and his affections from the days of Tone to those of Parnell, but you sold him to the enemy or failed him in need or reviled him and left him for another. And you invite me to be one of you. I'd see you damned first. (*A Portrait*, 207)

At this point of their conversation, there is a complete shift in the register of the dialogue.

> Stephen, following his own thought, was silent for an instant.
> – The soul is born, he said vaguely, first in those moments I told you of. It has a slow and dark birth, more mysterious than the birth of the body. When the soul of a man is born in this country there are nets flung at it to hold it back from flight. You talk to me of nationality, language, religion. I shall try to fly by those nets. . . .
> – Do you know what Ireland is? asked Stephen with cold violence. Ireland is the old sow that eats her farrow. (*A Portrait*, 207–8)

Interestingly, Stephen's cold violent invective against his country is placed in the very middle of his discussions on the nature of beauty, art, pity and terror. Aristotle and, especially, Aquinas are often mentioned. Finally, the aesthetic/poetic conversation with Lynch is brought to an end by the announcement: *Your beloved is here.*

The remaining section of *A Portrait* is crammed with ostensible references to Dante's *Vita Nuova*. For instance:

> Stephen took his place silently on the step below the group of students . . . turning his eyes towards her from time to time. She too stood silently among her companions. (220)
> He had written verses for her again after ten years . . . Ten years from that wisdom of children to his folly. (226)

> She passed out from the porch of the library and bowed across Stephen in reply to Cranly's greeting. (236)
> It was not thought nor vision though he knew vaguely that her figure was passing homeward through the city. Vaguely first and then more sharply he smelt her body. A conscious unrest seethed in his blood. (237–8) [11]

Finally, in the penultimate page of *A Portrait*, in the last encounter of the sweethearts, in this last fragment of Joyce's *Vita Nuova*, Dante Alighieri is explicitly mentioned, with an ambiguously ironic perhaps, yet somehow high-handed, remark.

> 15 April: Met her today pointblank in Grafton Street. The crowd brought us together. We both stopped. She asked me why I never came, said she had heard all sorts of stories about me. This was only to gain time. Asked me, was I writing poems? About whom? I asked her. This confused her more and I felt sorry and mean. Turned off that valve at once and opened the spiritual-heroic refrigerating apparatus, invented and patented in all countries by Dante Alighieri. Talked rapidly of myself and my plans. (256)

Here ends Joyce's *Vita Nuova*. Like Dante's *Vita Nuova*, *A Portrait* is the story of youthful desire sublimated and displaced in the artist's search for poetic identity.

'*A Portrait* is the story of a young artist who wants to write *A Portrait*',[12] just as Dante's *Vita Nuova* is, principally (and Joyce correctly read it as such), a well-structured system of poetic compositions by a poet who wants to say what poetry is. In *A Portrait*, behind the ostensible robust frame of Thomas Aquinas, as aesthetician and philosopher, hides – for Joyce – the inspiring presence of Dante, as inspired poet and master of poetic strategies, creative skills and artistic devices.

No doubt, the strong presence of aesthetic discourse and the lengthy analyses of Aquinas's definitions of beauty served the purpose of articulating Joyce's understanding of 'epiphany' and acted as substitute for *Stephen Hero*'s insights into the essence of epiphanic poetic vision. The central concern of the *Artist as a Young Man*, however, is no longer beauty but rather art. In this sense, Joyce concealed behind aesthetic categories the exploration of poetic devices and artistic creation. Aesthetic preoccupations are metamorphosed into poetic experimentation: Aquinas flows into and merges with Dante Alighieri, whose *Vita Nuova* is a celebration of Beatrice, of the poet's love for her and – at once – the blueprint of Dante's poetics or his conception and practice of poetry as art. In a similar manner, the real protagonist of *A Portrait* is not so much Stephen Dedalus alias young Jim as artist, but rather – behind Dedalus the artist/artificer – art itself and the process of artistic creation.

From his early student years, Joyce studied Dante and valued him more than any other poet. Only Homer and Shakespeare are as ubiquitously present in all his writings as Dante is. And Joyce had no hesitation in calling him 'the first poet of the Europeans'. In a lecture he gave in Trieste, in 1922, he went so far as to remark: 'Italian literature begins with Dante and finishes with Dante. That's more than a little. In Dante dwells the whole spirit of the Renaissance' (Ellmann, 226).

By elevating the *lingua volgare* to the power and dignity of high art, Dante has granted his successors a new tongue, he has given voice to a new culture and a new consciousness. Joyce set out to achieve no less, as we read in the final lines of *A Portrait*:

> 'Welcome, O life! I go to encounter for the millionth time the reality of experience and to forge in the smithy of my soul the uncreated conscience of my race.
>
> Old father, old artificer, stand me now and ever in good stead.'

(I have often wondered whether the final invocation was not actually intentionally addressed to the divine poet, the great exile from Florence).

In his plan to forge the uncreated conscience of his race, Joyce – 'the Dante of Dublin', as Oliver St John Gogarty and his student friends learnt to call him – was to remain close to the Florentine poet. As early as in 1905, Joyce saw the connection between his intentions and Dante's achievement. In a letter to his publisher, Grant Richards (*Letters* II, 122), he wrote:

I do not think that any writer has yet presented Dublin to the world. It has been a capital of Europe for thousands of years, it is supposed to be the second city of the British empire and it is nearly three times as big as Venice. Moreover, on account of many circumstances which I cannot detail here, the expression Dubliner seems to me to bear some meaning and I doubt whether the same can be said for such words as 'Londoner' and 'Parisian', both of which have been used by writers as titles.

We know, of course, that he was referring to his *Dubliners*. But we also sense a note of pride and of nostalgia for his 'fair sheepfold'. In his intention to become the poet of his race and the voice of his culture, Joyce planned nothing less than to make Dublin, as Dante made Florence, the centre and projection of a universal drama. *Ulysses* is precisely the realisation of this ambitious project.

Ulysses is, for modernity, what Dante's *Commedia* was for the Middle Ages and the Renaissance: not a *Divine Comedy*, for *Ulysses* knows no transcendence and in Joyce's poetic universe there is 'the absolute absence of the Absolute', but a fully temporal and human *Commedia*. Unlike Dante's cosmically ordered, transparent and closed universe, Joyce has articulated increasingly ambiguous narratives and given form to increasingly formless, chaotic, open worlds. Once again, we are confronted by yet another *coincidentia oppositorum* and 'identity of contraries'. This time, the *coincidentia* focuses on the problem of form, structure and system, at first, and on the problem of rhetorical strategies. Once again, the presence of Dante – and of Aquinas – emerges in the poetic world of Joyce. No doubt, during his years of study Jim must have become acquainted with the systematic and structured form of Medieval thought, aptly expressed in the architectonic construction of the *Summae* (Eco, 14–22). However, it was in Dante's *Commedia*: the large and complex allegorical poem in which the endless and vast variety of human experience is rigorously ordered within the formal frame of a perfectly organised structure, that Joyce found the prototypical order that inspired the formal solution to be adopted in the composition of *Ulysses*. The classical and Medieval world was conceived as ordered, finite and closed. The structure of the *Summae* like the symmetrical harmony of Dante's *Commedia* stand as tangible metaphors of their world-view. *Dubliners* and *A Portrait* represent a world as a microcosm that is closed and finite, yet already exhibiting signs of conflict, disorder and disruption. In *Ulysses*, the preoccupation with – and the need for – formal stability, becomes more cogent. And, with this, Dante's inspiration is also more strongly felt. In this work, the realistic observation and depiction of the characters, 'constitute only the *literal* dimension of a much vaster *allegorical* and *anagogical system*' (Eco, 33).

Not unlike *La Divina Commedia, Ulysses* was conceived by its maker as a *summa* of the universe.

As Joyce explained in one of his *Letters* (I, 146–7):

> It is an epic of two races (Israelite-Irish) and at the same time the cycle of the human body as well as a little story of a day (life). . . . It is also a sort of encyclopaedia. My intention is to transpose the myth *sub specie temporis nostri.* Each adventure (that is, every hour, every organ, every art being interconnected and interrelated in the structural scheme of the whole) should not only condition but even create its own technique.

The book is conceived of as a total work, a Work-as-Cosmos. Joyce adopts the formal structure of the classical order – as he found it in Aquinas and Dante, particularly – and superimposes it onto the experiential and existential world of disorder in which the contemporary artist is immersed. In the words of Umberto Eco:

> He has paradoxically superimposed the classical order onto the world of disorder which is accepted and recognized as the place of the contemporary artist. . . . *Ulysses* appears as the incredible image of a world that supports itself almost by miracle, on the preserved structures of an old world, which are accepted for their formal reliability but denied in their substantial value. *Ulysses* represents a moment of transition for contemporary sensibility. It appears as the drama of a dissociated consciousness that tries to reintegrate itself. . . . with *Ulysses* we can speak of a great epic of

the classical mode, like Dante's *Commedia*, conceived in Dublin rather than Florence. The book – which is really a model of itself – encompasses a grandiose mass of experience and the totality of the problems of contemporary culture. (Eco, 54–6)

The adoption of classical and Medieval formal order, the exploitation of allegorical narrative, the linguistic explorations and experimentations aimed at forging the uncreated conscience of his race: these poetic strategies deployed in *Ulysses* were to be further pursued in *Finnegans Wake*, to the extreme limit of possibility.

If *Ulysses* is an attempt at containing chaos within form, if it 'represents the most arduous attempt to give physiognomy to chaos, *Finnegans Wake* shamelessly defines itself as a *Chaosmos* and a *Microchasm*. and constitutes the most terrifying document of formal instability and semantic ambiguity that we possess'(Eco, 61). And if *Ulysses* could not be fully understood without reference to Dante, *Finnegans Wake* cannot be fully appreciated without reference to Nicholas of Cusa, Giordano Bruno and especially Giambattista Vico.

Vico

As Ellmann has recorded: 'when the Danish writer Tom Kristensen confessed that he needed help with *Finnegans Wake* (then known simply as *Work in Progress*), Joyce suggested a reading of Vico. "But do you believe in the

Scienza Nuova?" asked Kristensen. "I don't believe in any science," Joyce answered, "but my imagination grows when I read Vico as it doesn't when I read Freud and Jung".' (Ellmann, 706)

We must not fail to note that, in Joyce's answer, the opposition between science and imagination invokes a central idea in Vico's thought. References to Vico abound in *Ulysses*. We find mention of *Vico Road, Dalkey*, in the *Nestor* episode; we encounter – in the thunder 'black crack of noise' in the *Oxen of the Sun* episode – a suggestion to Vico's divine thunderclap; and at the end of the day Leopold Bloom thinks of 'the vogue of Dr. Tibble's Vi-Cocoa'.[13] Though present in *Ulysses*, Vico looms large on the chaotic nocturnal landscape of *Finnegans Wake*. In fact, he is announced at the very outset, twice in the first page of the work: firstly by name – standing, metonymically, for his theory of *corsi e ricorsi storici*:

> riverrun past Eve and Adam's, from swerve of shore to bend of bay, brings us by a commodius vicus of recirculation back to Howth Castle and Environs.

The second reference is indirect, yet far too obvious to be missed. It occurs with the onomatopoeic 'polygluttural' lengthy rendering of the thunder:

> bababadalgharaghtakamminarronnkonnbronntonnerronn-tuonntrovarrhounawnskawntoohoohoordenenthurnuk!

The name of Vico and the metonymically implied
reference to his philosophical theory of universal history,
refer – in turn – to the circular and cyclical structure of
the book: they announce the formal solution adopted by
Joyce, in order to paradoxically shape chaos in a chaoti-
cally cosmic manner. On the other hand, the multilingual
onomatopoeic rendering of the thunder, and the fear
of thunderstorms – which figures as a prominent and
recurrent theme in the work – lead us to a cluster of
interconnected ideas: the beginning of culture, the birth
of mythopoietic imagination, the beginning of the
heroic age of mankind, the discovery of metaphorical
language, the beginning of a new age . . . Joyce was
particularly impressed by Vico's powerful page on the
revelatory effect of thunder upon our brutish ancestors
(*bestioni*), also because of his own fear of thunder: a
fear that – shared with Vico – was instilled in him,
from childhood, by Dante's (this time Mrs Conway!)
superstitious, punitive, vengeful and super-ego version
of religion.

> Her piety affected him less than her superstition; she
> talked a good deal about the end of the world, as if she
> expected it at any moment, and when there was a flash of
> lightning she taught James to cross himself and say, 'Jesus
> of Nazareth, King of the Jews, from a sudden and
> unprovided for death deliver us, O Lord.' The thunder-
> storm as a vehicle of divine power and wrath moved Joyce's

imagination so profoundly that to the end of his life he trembled at the sound. When a friend asked him why he was so affected, he replied, 'You were not brought up in Catholic Ireland'. (Ellmann, 25)

For Vico the justification or the intelligibility of history is to be found in the nature of the human mind, which unfolds in a succession of developmental stages: sense experience, fantasy or imagination, reflective reason. These, in turn, inform three successive stages of historical progression: the age of the gods, the age of heroes, the age of rational humans. Hence, human beings 'first sense experience, without explicit awareness; then they become aware, with perturbed and moved hearts; finally they reflect with clear reason'. Vico suggests, therefore, that our primitive ancestors – at the dawn of mankind – experienced the world through 'most robust sensations and feelings', and expressed them 'by means of vast symbolic phantasies or images'. The primitive barbarism of a 'sensuous' humanity, after an age of heroic and poetic imagination, turns into the final phase of rationality and eventually of a new barbarism: the barbarism of reflection (*La scienza nuova,* par. 1106). This is Vico's theory of *corsi e ricorsi*: historical ebb and flow, flux and re-flux, cycles and re-cycles or repetitions.

In his attempt to throw light on the very origin of the human world, and in order to resolve the opposition between spontaneity and reflection, feeling and knowledge, art and philosophy, imagination and science, Vico articulated the idea of 'poetic wisdom' (*Scienza Nuova*, Libro II). The primitive world, inhabited first by 'bestioni' (brutes), inarticulate like infants, then by giants, finally by heroic races; is the world of humanity in its childhood: a world ruled by sensuous and imaginative spontaneity. This is the age of 'poetic wisdom': wisdom, in so far as our ancestors grasped the essence of reality; poetic, because truth was presented and articulated not through reflection but in the shape of images, myths, poems, metaphors, art. Vico's idea of 'poetic wisdom' is akin to Joyce's idea of 'epiphany', and corresponds to what we call 'visual thinking'.[14]

In Vico's more detailed map of the historical development of mankind we soon encounter Homer, no longer presumed to be an individual poet, but rather seen as a heroic type symbolising a collective consciousness. Joyce found Vico's understanding of history, of poetic wisdom and of the Homeric problem quite congenial and attractive. Hence, for Joyce, 'history "moves in vicous cicles yet remewes the same"' (*Finnegans Wake*, 134, 16–17), and his archetypal hero, Humphrey Chimpden Earwicker, constantly re-enacts the basic patterns of behaviour which apply to all men in all ages'.[15]

For Vico the beginning of humanity was marked by an experience of awakening. The primitive humans, stultified brutes after Adam's fall, were suddenly shaken out of their state of brutish stupidity. And this happened – as Vico suggests in one of his most robust pages – when the first thunderclap shook the monotony of the sky after the flood.

> And they, frightened and terrified by the powerfully horrendous noise of which they knew not the cause, raised their eyes and saw the sky.

Joyce must have found this idea attractive, intriguing and quite memorable, also because of his own fear of lightning and thunderclaps, which – as we have noted – he shared with Vico. And he toyed with Vico's view of a naturalistic and animistic religious sentiment of awe that was at the origin of the human world, and its symbolic connection with the thunderbolt that comes from the sky. Furthermore, he paid homage to Vico – albeit in an ironical manner – when, frightened by a thunderbolt, he answered to a friend's observation that his children were not afraid of the thunderstorm: 'They have no religion'.[16]

The incipient religious sentiment, in turn, is – according to the Neapolitan philosopher – first articulated through mytho-poetic discourse. Poetry, myths, tales, sagas tell us the story of our origins. They constitute a special kind of pictorial metaphysics or a kind of 'visual thinking'. Vico was obsessed with this idea, to which he referred as the *universale fantastico*. To this is also connected Vico's idea of the origin of language.

We find that the principle of the origins of languages and letters lies in the fact that the first gentile peoples, by a demonstrated necessity of nature, were poets who spoke in poetic characters.

Vico refers to this 'discovery' as 'the master key of this Scienza Nuova'. The language of poetry and myth, that forges the character and the identity of a race, operates by exploiting the global system of rhetorical figures: tropes, metaphors, poetic images, etymologies, onomatopoeas, that fundamentally defy conventional syntactic and semantic rules of linguistic articulation.

With this we come – almost! – to identify fully the presence of Vico in *Finnegans Wake*. We know that Joyce read Vico, at first through the mediation of Quinet, Michelet and Croce. And he cleverly – once again! – manages to compress and 'condense' (in a cryptic and allusive manner) the names of Quinet, Michelet, Vico and Bruno in a much studied passage of Book I.

> From quiqui quinet to michemiche chelet and a jambe-batiste to a brulobrulo! It is told in sounds in utter that, in signs so adds to, in universal, in polygluttural, in each ausiliary neutral idiom, sordomutics, florilingua, sheltafo-cal, flayflutter, a con's cubane, a pro's tutute, strassarab, ereperse and anythong athall. (117)

This passage illustrates the chaotic polyvalence of *Finnegans Wake*'s language and the fundamental defiance of conventional linguistic rules.

Joyce's dialogue with the Neapolitan philosopher focused mainly on two central ideas: the cyclical model of historical development and – more significantly – the origin and nature of poetic language. With reference to the first idea, W.Y. Tindall has outlined the general design of *Finnegans Wake* in the following terms:

Finnegans Wake is divided into four books, the first three long and the last one short. The first book has eight chapters, the second and third books have four chapters apiece, and the fourth has one chapter. The first book is Vico's divine age, the second his heroic age, and the third his human age. The fourth book is the reflux that leads to the divine again. In the first book we occupy a gigantic and fabulous world, but since subsequent history grows out of this world, the elements of the later ages are present in it. Each book contains the elements of the others, and each book contains the whole pattern. Each chapter of each book is one of Vico's ages. In Book I the first four chapters represent a complete cycle with its reflux. The second four chapters repeat the cycle on another level. The four chapters of Book II and the four chapters of Book III constitute two more cycles. Joyce indicated the end of a cycle by the word Silence. This word occurs in the third chapters of Book II and Book III before the reflux. The main structure, therefore, is one large cycle, containing four smaller cycles.[17]

Of the cyclical structure of *Finnegans Wake* and on Vico's presence in the work, A. Walton Litz has noted that:

> 'Howth Castle and Environs,' the geographical centre of the book, conceals the initials of Joyce's hero, H. C. E. – both the landscape and the hero are reconstituted as we move along Vico's road, 'a commodius vicus of recirculation.' In a letter explaining the opening lines of *Finnegans Wake* Joyce glossed the phrase 'passencore rearrived' as the '*ricorsi storici* of Vico'. (*Letters* I, 248)[18]

The attention paid to Viconian cycles in *Finnegans Wake* should not make us insensitive to or unaware of the other, perhaps more important, subject of dialogue between Joyce and Vico; namely Vico's and Joyce's understanding and treatment of language. Joyce was acutely aware of living in an age 'which had witnessed the "abnihilisation of the etym" (353, 22), and he believed it was the job of the artist to build a new world of language out of the ruins of the old'. (Litz, 252)[19] In Eco's words:

> From the beginning, *Finnegans Wake* announces what it will be – a nocturnal epic of ambiguity and metamorphoses, the myth of a death and universal rebirth, in which each figure and each word will stand in the place of all the others. It will be an epic without clear divisions between the events, so that each event may implicate the others to form an elementary unity that does not exclude the collision and opposition between contraries. (Eco, 62)

This work – which I like to read as a metaphor of metaphors, a myth of myths, and a pun of puns – is structured cyclically and circularly, unendingly opening itself to itself, in an ever new re-enactment of itself, unendingly folding itself upon itself. It is a global image of the universe and of language, a map of nature metamorphosed into culture. As such, *Finnegans Wake* is the ideal book intended for the 'ideal reader suffering from an ideal insomnia'. As a frightfully ambiguous and almost hallucinatory 'open work', 'it defines itself as a *scherzarade* (a game, a scherzo, a charade, an endless tale of Sheherazade) a *vicocyclometer*, a *collideoscope*, a work of *double-crossing twofold truths and devising tail-words*'. (Eco, 66)

A great epiphany of the universe resolved into language, *Finnegans Wake* – as the exemplary *summa* of avant-garde poetics – is the poetics of itself. By the same token, it signals the birth of a new type of discourse: the language of *Chaosmos*. In Joyce's dialogue with Vico we witness yet another *coincidentia oppositorum*. The Neapolitan philosopher looked at history, language and poetry, seeking an underlying order and design. Joyce transformed history, myth and language into a cyclical recurrence of chaos.

In a parallel manner, as Umberto Eco has suggested, Dante's project for the establishment of a perfect tongue, in his *De Vulgari Eloquentia* – consisted in finding a language that would allow mankind's escape from the post-babelic labyrinth. A perfect tongue, however, should be clear, perspicuous and not labyrinthine. On the contrary, Joyce's project, as he progressively moved from his early Thomistic aesthetics to the world-vision expressed by *Finnegans Wake*, is really about overcoming the post-babelic confusion by *accepting and exploiting it*. Joyce did not try to go before or beyond the Tower, but rather wanted to live *inside it*. (See pp. 19–20 above)

Svevo

Having travelled – hopefully, not too un-commodiously – the vicus-path that led us from Dedalus's Irish and autobiographical microcosm to the galactic nebula of chaosmic (or chaos-cosmic?) language, let us return to the umbilical place of Joyce's universe and to its central protagonists. I mean, obviously, the *Ulysses* universe and its leading actors: Stephen and Leopold, with Molly – of course – to complete the trinitarian schema. (I am not aware of any contextual and intertextual investigation on Molly, the trinity and the tower.)

An account of the formation of these characters – especially Stephen (a son in search of a father, and new Telemachus) still wrestling with life from the distance of literature's vantage point, and Leopold Bloom (new Ulysses, wandering Jew and a father in search of a son) – would be quite incomplete without reference to Joyce's

Triestine dialogue with Ettore Schmitz and his wife Livia Veneziani.

In 1907 Schmitz – the industrialist whose firm successfully produced and exported a high quality, long lasting, protective paint for ships, and had expanded to the extent of opening a branch in Great Britain – looked for a private tutor of English. He found James Joyce. It was a momentous encounter for both teacher and pupil. In no time their relationship outgrew the bounds of professional exchange, to become sincere – though formal and respectful – friendship, and later to mature into mutual recognition for their respective literary work and worth. That mutual acknowledgement triggered and sustained a substantial dialogue and provided reciprocal spiritual sustenance.

We are told that, also because of the advanced proficiency of the pupils Ettore and Livia, Joyce's lessons mostly consisted of conversation and improvised literary exercises. One of the favourite topics was Joyce's own writings. 'Late in 1907 he read the Schmitzes "The Dead", which he had recently completed. After the reading Livia went down into the garden to pick a bouquet and offered it to him in homage.'[20]

Duly impressed with Joyce's literary ability and perceiving in his writing a congenial sensibility, Schmitz picked up courage and lent his tutor – and now comrade in arms – two books he had already published, *Una*

Vita and *Senilità*, without receiving any critical recognition. That same evening, Jim told Stanislaus: 'Schmitz has given me two novels of his to read. I wonder what kind of thing it is'. Obviously, Joyce's expectations were not very high. For this reason, his surprise was all the greater. He was intrigued by the two novels which he read voraciously. At the following meeting, two days later, Joyce told Svevo that he had been unjustly ignored and neglected. He went so far as to say that in *Senilità* there were pages that Anatole France could not have written better. Furthermore, Joyce proceeded with quoting by heart selected pages and passages. Svevo was thrilled, much encouraged, comforted and gratified. As he resumed, with renewed confidence, his creative writing, he at once returned Joyce's favour by assuming the role of listener, reader, mentor and moral supporter of his young friend. Joyce, more connected – especially in his later Zürich and Paris years – with the official literary world, introduced and promoted Svevo's talent among leading literary and editorial figures. Svevo, for his part, counselled Joyce with criticism, observations, encouragement and recognition. In the Triestine years, previous to Joyce's migration to Zürich, Svevo remained his only close writer-friend.

At first sight – and considering their respective outward physiognomy – we can only find differences between Svevo and Joyce. In fact, any kind of congenial relationship between the two would appear highly improbable. To begin with, they differed in age by some twenty years. Joyce was a young bohemian of 25 years when they met. Svevo was a middle-aged respectable bourgeois, a wealthy and successful industrialist. Joyce was penniless and still very much in the making: arrogant and eccentric. Svevo was humble and conservative. Joyce was extroverted and self-centred, Svevo was self-doubting, thoughtful and benevolent. Joyce was witty, but often sarcastic. Svevo had *Witz* and tremendous psychological insight into the human heart. Though equally endowed with ironic disposition and the ability to observe the weird oddness of existence, they differed in their respective reading of the human psyche: in Joyce one feels a pervasive sense of distantly impending despair, in Svevo the apparent futility of the human condition is softened by deep empathy and compassion.

Of course, they came from completely different cultural backgrounds and were raised in quite different environments. 'Svevo grew up in a well-to-do Jewish family; Joyce in a relatively poor Irish Catholic one. Although he was well educated, Svevo never experienced the strict intellectual and moral discipline that was a substantial part of Joyce's training at the Jesuit schools.' Svevo was raised in a free-thinking world, as opposed to the provincial world of the microcosmic Dublin which Joyce despised and finally fled as a young man.[21]

Behind and beyond these ostensible and obvious differences, however, deeper similarities must be noted: common artistic and literary traits that these two great cartographers of the modern soul shared. Joyce had shaped his literary identity at the school of Aquinas, Dante, Ibsen and the French Symbolists, finally to narrate an epic story of quotidian banal human condition and of human alienation in a disjointed world and in the chaos of language. Svevo – familiar with Middle-European literature, especially Kafka – wrote to overcome the stagnant condition of the Italian literary tradition, by ironically depicting the decay of bourgeois existence, capturing the most minute traits and twitches of the psyche. Both exploited the technique of the inward/inword monologue. Both worked at the reconstitution of human experience, utilising the bits and pieces, the fragments left at their disposal: Joyce, manipulating the fragments of autobiography, of a city and of language; Svevo, focusing on the psychic fragments caught in the flow of the stream of consciousness. Both exploited the unconscious hallucinatory discourse of free association, even though Svevo understood and acknowledged the logic of dream-formation, while Joyce pretended no interest and no insight into psychoanalytic concern with the unconscious.

We know that Joyce learnt much about Jewish customs from Svevo who once told Stanislaus: 'Tell me some secrets about Irishmen. You know your brother has been asking so many questions about Jews that I want to get even with him.' In the introduction to the English translation of *Senilità,* Stanislaus was later to write: 'It may not be too far-fetched to see in the person of Bloom Svevo's maturer, objective, peaceable temper reacting upon the young man's fiery mettle'.

Even though Joyce picked up traits of his Leopold Bloom also from another Jewish acquaintance in Trieste, Svevo's friend Teodoro Mayer (editor of the newspaper *Il Piccolo,* for which Joyce was asked to write), there is an unmistakable echo of Jim's feelings towards Svevo, in the relationship between Stephen Dedalus and Leopoldo/ Teodoro Bloom.

In the intricate and rich network of connections established by Joyce's dialogue with Svevo, we must mention – to conclude – that which links Svevo's wife to the Joycean universe. We must note, to begin, that Livia Veneziani Svevo, in her *Vita di mio marito*: a biograph-ical portrait of Svevo, mentions frequently – and always with friendly affection and admiration – Joyce's name, deeds and literary achievements.

The connection with Livia is now immortalised in *Finnegans Wake*'s mythical name of the river Liffey: Anna Livia Plurabelle. On 21 November 1925, Joyce wrote to Svevo:

Reassure your wife with regard to Anna Livia. I have taken no more than her hair from her and even that only on loan, to adorn the rivulet which runs through my city, the Anna Liffey, which would be the longest river in the world if it weren't for the canal which comes from far away to wed the divine Antonio Taumaturgo, and then changing its mind, goes back the way it came.[22]

In later years, Joyce explained to an enquiring journalist:

They say I have immortalised Svevo, but I've also immortalised the tresses of Signora Svevo. These were long and reddish-blond. My sister who used to see them let down told me about them. There is a river near Dublin which passes dye-houses and its waters are reddish, so I've enjoyed comparing these two things in the book I'm writing. A lady in it will have the tresses which are really Signora Svevo's.

In 1939, on New Year's Day, Joyce wrote to Livia Svevo, to announce the completion of *Finnegans Wake*:

Dear Signora: I have at last finished finishing my book. For three lustra I have been combing and recombing the locks of Anna Livia. It is now time that she tread the board.

And so riverrunning along the stream of the combed and recombed hair of Anna Livia Plurabelle, the commodius vicus that from Dublin's bend of bay led us to Florence, Naples, Trieste, takes us finally back to where we started from.

For Joyce, Trieste was an extension of the Dublin streets, an echo of Dublin sounds and, as Svevo put it: 'A stretch of Ireland which had grown ripe in the sun'. There, in dialogue with Aquinas, Dante, Bruno, Vico, Svevo, our Dublin hero also grew ripe in the sun. Combing and re-combing, fluxing and re-fluxing, cycling and re-cycling, in Trieste James Joyce – the Dante of Dublin, the Bruno the Nolan, the vicocyclometer – had once occupied a flat near a square where the Svevo/Schmitz family owned a house. By a wonderful coincidence, the name of the square is . . . Piazza Giambattista Vico!

Notes

1. In *Our Exagmination round his Factification for Incamination of Work in Progress*. Paris: Shakespeare & Company, 1929. As is well known, the dots that follow each name in the title stand for the number of centuries that separated one writer from the next.
2. Ellmann, Richard, *James Joyce*. New and Revised Edition. Oxford University Press, 1983, pp. 228–9. I shall refer to this, in the text, by writing: (Ellmann, page number).
3. We can think, in the spirit of Joyce's playful observation and following the logic of his toying with words, of . . . Marcelli, Rutelli, Bernardelli, Rossini, Bellini, Puccini, Boccherini, Cherubini, Scaramuzzi, Andreucci, Petrucci, Fantuzzi, Bertolucci, Censini, Fellini, Cenciarelli, Cenerilli, Franceschini, Feltrinelli, Fiorini, Fiorilli, Botticelli, Barberini – and, since we are getting close to Via Frattina – why not also Borromini and Bernini?. . . .

4. A degree of spiteful feeling towards the immortal city is also to be found in *A Portrait of the Artist as a Young Man*, where Stephen's friend Temple says: 'Hell is Roman, like the walls of the Romans, strong and ugly'. (The definitive text, corrected from the Dublin holograph by Chester G. Anderson and edited by Richard Ellmann. London: Jonathan Cape, 1968, p. 241. Any future reference to *A Portrait etc.*, will be to this edition and it will be indicated, in the text, by the abbreviation: *A Portrait*, followed by the page number).

5. Perhaps Joyce understood well that, for Dante, the greatest sin is that against trust. And perhaps also for this reason he adopted the posture of one who had been betrayed by the whole of humanity, by his country, by his religion, by his friends, with a few exceptions – so that he could happily place any and each of his alleged 'traitors' in the hell/purgatory of his imagination.

6. *Letters of James Joyce*, Vol. II, Ed. Richard Ellmann, New York: Viking, 1966, p. 168.

7. *Paradiso* XVII, 55–60

8. Praz, Mario, 'Introduzione', *J. Joyce, Ritratto dell'artista da giovane*. Roma: Newton Compton Italiana, 1973, p. 16.

9. Paris, Jean, 'James Joyce par lui-même', in *Écrivains de toujours*. Paris: Éditions du Seuil, 1957.

10. Tr. by H.F. Cary, *The Divine Comedy of Dante*. London: J.M. Dent & Sons, 1908.

11. Also to identify Joyce's intertextual games and precise references to Dante, see Mary T. Reynolds's excellent study: *Joyce and Dante. The Shaping Imagination*. Princeton: Princeton University Press, 1981.

12. Eco, Umberto, *The Aesthetics of Chaosmos. The Middle Ages of James Joyce*. Tulsa: The University of Tulsa, 1982, p. 1. Future references to this delightful, inspiring and magisterial study will be indicated in the text by: (Eco, followed by page number).

13. It has also been convincingly suggested that the whole *Nestor* episode re-enacts, quite rigorously, the four-part Vichian cycle of history's ages: age of the gods – age of heroes – age of men – finally the Ricorso. See: A.M., Klein, 'A Shout in the Street', *New Directions in Prose and Poetry*, 1951, No.13, p. 331. I must also clarify that, although Joyce uses Vico Road as a reference to and a resonance of the philosopher's name, the topographic name of the Dalkey road, near Dublin, derives directly from the name of a small town in the gulf of Naples, near Sorrento: Vico Equense.

14. On the theme of metaphor and 'visual thinking', see Dorfles, Gillo, 'Myth and Metaphor in Vico and in Contemporary Aesthetics', in Giorgio Tagliacozzo (Ed.), *Giambattista Vico. An International Symposium.* Baltimore: The Johns Hopkins Press, 1969, pp. 577–90.

15. Litz, A. Walton, 'Vico and Joyce', in G. Tagliacozzo (Ed.), *Op. cit.*, p. 251.

16. The connection of thunder to religious feelings (of fear) – hence, reference to Vico – is made in Molly Bloom's monologue: '. . .yes because I felt lovely and tired myself and fell asleep as sound as a top the moment I popped straight into bed till that thunder woke me up as if the world was coming to an end God be merciful to us I thought the heavens were coming down about us to punish us when I blessed myself and said a Hail Mary like those awful thunderbolts in Gibraltar and they come and tell you theres no God. . .'.

17. Tindall, W. Y., *James Joyce: His Way of Interpreting the Modern World.* New York, 1950, p. 72.

18. Litz, A. Walton, *Op. cit.*, p. 252.

19. On the wide and fertile theme of Vico's conception of language and its influence on Joyce, see in particular the quoted studies by Umberto Eco and A. Walton Litz. It is worth noting that

Beckett shared Joyce's attraction to Vico's conception of language, myth and poetry, as primitive and pre-rational phenomena.

20. Furbank, P. N., *Italo Svevo. The Man and the Writer.* London: Secker & Warburg, 1978, p. 81. The occasion, by the way, is recorded – with a tone of touching tenderness – by Livia Veneziani in the biography of her husband.

21. Rocco-Bergera, N., 'Joyce and Svevo: A Note', *Modern Fiction Studies,* Vol. 18, No. 1, 1972, pp. 116–17.

22. *Letters of James Joyce.* Vol III, ed. Richard Ellmann, London: Faber & Faber, 1966, p. 133. The original text, in Italian, of part of this letter to Ettore Schmitz, alias Italo Svevo, runs as follows: 'Rassicuri la Sua Signora in quanto riguarda la figura d'Anna Livia. Di lei non tolsi che la capigliatura e quella soltanto e prestito per addobbare il rigagnolino della mia città l'Anna Liffey che sarebbe il più lungo fiume del mondo se non ci fosse il canal che viene da lontano per sposare il gran divo, Antonio Taumaturgo e poi cambiato parere se ne torna com' è venuto.' This message echoes a previous message, of 20 February 1924, to the same addressee, where Joyce asked for permission to make reference – in *Finnegans Wake* – to Livia's hair. 'A propos of names: I have given the name of Signora Schmitz to the protagonist of the book I am writing. Ask her, however, not to take up arms, either of steel or fire, since the person involved is the Pyrrha of Ireland (or rather of Dublin) whose hair is the river beside which (her name is Anna Liffey) the seventh city of Christianity springs up, the other six being Bassovizza, Clapham Junction, Rena Vecia, Limehouse, S. Odorico in the Vale of Tears and San Giacomo in Monte di Pietà.' *Letters of James Joyce.* Ed. Stuart Gilbert, London: Faber & Faber, 1957, pp. 211–12.